76 Ways

to Build a Straight Referral Business- ASAP!

By Lorna Riley, CSP

 An Off-the-Chart™ Publication

Off-the-Chart Publications
2455 Flametree Lane
Vista, CA 92084
tel 760-639-4020
fax 760-639-4023

www.lornariley.com
Lorna@lornariley.com

Printed in the United States of America

76 Ways

Table of Contents

Page:

76 Ways Listing

Check off the most appropriate ideas for your business:

TECHNIQUES

Page #

ATTITUDES

Introduction

Imagine a day in which the phone is ringing off the hook with qualified buyers asking for you by name! If you're ready to do more business in less time, work smarter not harder, and increase your income, then referrals are the way to go.

I've used the ideas in this book to increase my sales productivity by 600%. You'll find practical tools that you can use *now* to increase your bottom line. Referrals are the most powerful strategy for increasing income because they compress sales time. They connect you with more qualified buyers, generate more call backs, and allow more "yeses" in less time.

"Refer" means to direct to a source for help or information. In *76 Ways* the word "referrals" means any names or contact information you're given for the purposes of doing business. These are people who may or may not know you, but the one thing they have in common is that they need your product or services. Referrals work both ways—they're either given *to you* by other people, or given *by you* to other people.

Referral ━━━▶ You   Referral ◀━━━ You

Here are three important truths about referrals:

1. Referrals are a dividend on superior service.
If you provide excellent service to others, you've not only earned the right to ask for referrals, but others will be more inclined to offer them to you. People are naturally eager to talk with others about products and services that have helped them to solve problems. It's called "work of mouth." Go the extra mile in quality service and people will be lining up to do business with you.

1

2. Referrals are a "close in advance."

Even though a referral is a more qualified lead than a traditional "cold call," it's still a starting point. The lead still needs to be qualified for interest, feasibility, decision-making authority, and economic buying power. The difference is that with a referral, you enter the sales event with the endorsement of another person. That testimonial is priceless. Eventually, some referrals will bear fruit and you'll be able to close the sale. Think of every referral as a potential "close" in advance.

3. People tend to refer others "up."

Most people want to be liked, respected, and appreciated by others. This means that referring sources tend to refer people who are a positive reflection on them. In other words, they refer you to those with whom they are proud to be associated. What begins to happen is a stair step pattern, constantly being referred to higher, more influential levels. You may start out over the kitchen table, but you'll eventually find your way into the boardrooms of movers and shakers. Since not all referrals are qualified to buy, as more come your way you can become more selective, investing your time with the better, more qualified leads. If you want to get into big-ticket sales, you'll save a ton of time and frustration if you do it with referrals.

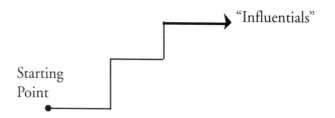

"Influentials"

Starting
Point

The most common ways to build referrals are to network or ask for them. The majority of business and sales professionals, however, do neither. They go about their day hoping that a few will trickle in. As you can tell from the title of this book they're short changing themselves everyday. There are literally dozens of strategies you can use. The point of this book is to bring as many ways as possible between two covers and to create measurable successes for you in the shortest period of time—ASAP! Many people who've used these ideas have started working on straight referrals within three weeks. *You can too!*

The ideas here are plentiful but brief by design. My experience has been that what a thick book offers in explanation takes away from you in time. I don't want you spending weeks reading this book, but rather years living with it and off it. These suggestions have a better chance of making a difference if you can get through them quickly and put the suggestions to work now!

I've created this book to be read with a pencil, asking for you to answer questions and personalize how you'll incorporate the ideas into your business. Unless you take action now, you'll forget about 80% of what you've read within the first 24 hours. If you wait a week, you may never get started. But if you employ one new idea each week, your productivity may increase by at least 10% each month. At that rate, by the end of the year you'll increase your productivity by 120%! That's an excellent ROI in anybody's book.

76 Ways is organized into three sections—techniques, attitudes, and an opportunity to test your knowledge. You can employ techniques but if your attitude's in the way, you'll be stumped before you get started. You must sincerely want

3

√

to work on referrals in order for the ideas to work for you. Sales has been called "the ability to control emotions until you find someone who wants to buy." If you can get negative emotions such as fear or reluctance out of the way, the flood-gates will open. Whenever you see this symbol:

it's me coaching you with an idea. Keep going and the going will get easier!

The ideas here are also presented in no particular priority order. Go through the book once, checking off the most appropriate ideas for your type of business, and then set goals to implement each one in your daily routine. Some will require more time to implement than others. Start with the simple ones and then build to the larger strategies.

The ideas are also very targeted to build your bottom line, but are founded on the principle that *you gain by giving*. The more you give of yourself to others in the way of service, caring, and commitment, the more you'll get back in return. This one concept is infused throughout the book. Whenever you find an idea that appears heavily promotional, the intent is always to extend what you do to a larger audience, allowing you to serve more people.

My goal for you is to enjoy unlimited success while working less. I want to close the gap between where you are and where you want to be, between the time you put down the book and pick up your bottom line—so let's get started!

You will get everything you want
when you increase your contribution to others.

Section 1
TECHNIQUES

1. Be Strategic

This entire book is about strategy so let's begin by defining what it is. Strategy is the plan you create to achieve a desired result. Since everything you do produces a result, having a strategic plan increases the probability that you'll achieve what you want not by default, but by design.

A strategic plan is your first step because it names what you want and how to get it. Desired results come from a dedicated, sometimes fanatical attention to a carefully chosen direction. You're either planning your life or others are, and they're often very misguided about what's right for you.

Strategy provides one critical, overarching benefit in obtaining referrals: *focus.* If you have no business focus, your referral results will be all over the map. I know a few people with just about every license imaginable—they can sell you real estate, insurance policies, broker loans, broker stock and do your taxes all under one roof. Most people are reluctant to refer anyone who's not a specialist. To get referrals, get good at what you do and get focused. To get focused, answer the question:

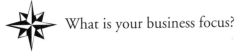 What is your business focus?

If you spread yourself too thin, your referrals will be too. Referral sources simply won't be able to associate you with any specialized area in which they feel confident about your talents and abilities.

5

How to Determine Your Business Focus:

Focus allows you to target your effort into the high-payoff areas offering the biggest return on your time investment. Business focus types falls into one of five categories. Check off the *one* area that you feel best describes your focus:

1. **People Focused:**

   Recognize an unmet want and seek ways of fulfilling that want. Design products and services *with* people, not *for* people.

   Nike targets a specific group of people such as athletes and then bombards them with new product lines that meet their unique needs. Customers talk about Nike to like-minded people because they value how their products perform in that niche—sports enthusiasts.

   To obtain referrals in this category, focus on co-creating products and services *with* people who have very specific related interests.

2. **Product Focus:**

   Make something first and then go out to see how many people want it. Insurance policies, homes, cell phones, gadgets and inventions of all kind are in this category. There's always an interest in innovative products and services that solve explicit or implicit problems.

   To obtain referrals in this area, focus on finding people with similar problems who do not need a highly customized solution.

6

3. Technological Focus:

Control a unique and valued technological process or idea. Look for products to which you can apply your technology, and then identify people or organizations that want this combined technology/product.

3M has a technology for bonding and coating which is useless by itself. When combined with products such as paper or plastic, something useful comes to life—adhesive tape, Post-It notes, fabric protection, weather stripping and more.

To obtain referrals in this area, find innovative ways of applying your technology to existing resources. Brainstorm with others to stimulate new applications for your technology.

4. Production Capability Focus:

Keep all assets running at peak capacity. The hospitality industry must pay for fixed costs every day (staff salaries, utility bills, food, landscaping maintenance, etc.) regardless of how many guests occupy the building. In order for hotels/motels to make a profit, they must fill rooms with people and run at full capacity every day. Steel and paper mills, airlines, restaurants, amusement parks, and movie theaters are also in this category.

To obtain referrals in this area, look for large groups of people who can help keep you running at full capacity.

5. **Distribution Focus:**
Build distribution channels as the core of your business. Using any one of a number of distribution vehicles, you sell appropriate products and services to that system for distribution to the people who use it.

Most multi-level marketing organizations are distribution focused. They sell products and services by recruiting distributors who in turn go out into the world to sell it on behalf of the manufacturer.

To obtain referrals in this area, look for people who are:
   a. willing to warehouse products
   b. sold on the value of the company or its products and services
   c. unwilling to make product themselves
   d. seeking income without the hassle of starting from "scratch"
   e. entrepreneurial-minded

Focus is the first step for creating a sound strategic foundation. Find your focus, let others know what it is, and STICK WITH IT!

 You are right where you need to be. Keep up the good work!

2. Define Your VP: Value Proposition

I call selling "creating perceived value." We buy and refer based on what we perceive to be of worth, whether there's any inherent value in the product or service itself. Value exists in the eyes of the beholder and is therefore transient. What we value today may be gone tomorrow. Selling means finding what others value *now* and then *proposing that value.*

Strategic business focus describes the inward attention needed to build one's capability and capacity, while your VP (value proposition) helps provide the external payoff from building that strength. Getting a college education, for example, is useful (focus), but it only pays off when that knowledge is applied externally to the world (value proposition).

There are five universal "VP's." Every person or organization worth its salt should offer *all* of them, but *specialize* in one. These propositions are quality, speed, low cost, service, and innovation. The one you choose as your "front runner" must be powerful enough to provide you with a distinctive imprint in the minds of others. The supporting four need only be at par with industry averages.

People buy from you over your competition because they prefer your primary VP *at that moment.* That value could change on a dime so timing is critical. As a result, customer loyalty is becoming more rare. Values are fickle and so are buying habits. To be sure that you understand the *current* values of your prospects, ask every time—assume nothing. We'll be covering this in more detail later, but for now check off the one category that best describes your primary VP.

9

1. **Quality:**

   People are willing to pay more for quality. Organizations pay tens of thousands of dollars more for highly experienced or well-educated talent. People pay small fortunes for high-end products like jewelry, luxury homes, or automobiles. Those who can't afford a big splurge may treat themselves to a quality small indulgence like a Monte Blanc pen.

2. **Speed:**

   People who can get their products or services to others faster than anyone else capture the attention of those who value speed. Federal Express built an empire by moving mail faster than the competition—the US mail.

3. **Low Cost:**

   Low cost offers attract price shoppers. Everyone likes a "deal," but those who value price over all else will walk if they don't hear the magic number, even if the quality is superior. The challenge to low cost as a primary value proposition is in competing with products and services that offer low cost *as well as* quality and service. If you sell your services below competitive rates, you'll attract those who consistently want the "best" deal no matter what the quality.

4. **Service:**

   This proposition must dazzle people with extraordinary service. 24-hour roadside assistance, or 24-hour help hot lines, or 24-hour convenience stores all present service as their edge. If you value service over all else, you'll seek ways to provide it better than anyone else. You'll "sense and respond" to needs before people even know that they want it. Hotels provide more in-room services such as free coffee, free newspapers, ironing boards, irons, bottled water, fax machines, internet hook ups, pay-per-view movies and snack bars. One hotel I stayed in greatly impressed me when the room service employee asked if I wanted to place a wake-up call with my dinner order.

5. Innovation:

People who offer innovation and creativity promise state-of-the-art, cutting edge products or ideas that cannot be acquired anywhere else. Hewlett-Packard uses innovation to be top of mind in the printer business. Artists, inventors, writers, and designers generally offer innovation as their primary VP. Innovation and creativity are arguably the most sought-after organizational VPs today.

Once you've identified your primary VP, you can help others to differentiate you from the competition. Teach your prospects and customers what makes you special.

When others are looking for your products and services, your contacts will be able to refer you as the one resource who *best* offers the value that they're looking for at that moment.

> *If you believe that your reason for being*
> *is to enlarge the lives of others,*
> *so too will your life be enlarged.*
> *Only then will the things you have learned to*
> *worry about take care of themselves.*

11

3. Be Value-Added

This concept spins off your VP value proposition. Being value-added is not a new idea, but it's also not being fully utilized. Value-added means answering:

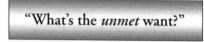

"What's the *unmet* want?"

If you can determine what people secretly want and aren't getting, you've taken a giant leap toward providing not only your primary value proposition, but also the *extra* value that will further set you apart from your competition.

Conduct a survey to assess how your customers currently perceive your business value. Can you offer extended hours, eliminate waiting, provide more one-on-one assistance, free consultation, one-click shopping on the web, or better products at a lower price? Are you ready to respond to customer needs quickly and efficiently? Customers value:

Convenience	Reliability	Honesty	Promptness
Accuracy	Cleanliness	Courtesy	Flexibility
Status	Recognition	Security	Saving Money

What others can you think of? _____

_____

Call your top ten most valued customers right now. Ask them what they value most about doing business with you. Then ask, "If there was *one* thing that I could do (or offer), that I'm not currently doing (offering), what would it be?" Tell them that you value their input. Don't let them off the hook if they say, "Everything's fine." If you want to improve, you have to ask questions that will help you identify hidden customer values. If you ask, "How's everything going?" you'll probably hear, "Fine." If you want better answers, ask better questions. Always be on the lookout for customer value clues. Then make it a goal to systematically integrate each value-added service/product into your business.

What value-added extras could you offer your customers?

_____

_____

_____

Each and every single day,
help someone in a value-added way.

4. Work the Law of 250

Joe Girard was named the top car salesman in America for 11 straight years, winning him entrance into the *Guinness Book of World Records*. In his book, *How to Sell Anything to Anybody*, he says that one of the most important principles he used for his sales success and building referrals was his "Law of 250."

After attending a number of weddings and funerals, Girard discovered that, "everyone knows 250 people in his or her life willing to attend their wedding or funeral." He reasoned that if he saw 50 people a week, but two of them were unhappy with his treatment, by the end of the year there would be about 5,000 people negatively influenced by just those two a week. Since he had been selling cars for 14 years, at that rate he would have angered about 70,000 people—enough to fill an entire stadium.

If the average person has 250 people close enough to be in their "inner circle," think of the thousands of direct and indirect contacts for those whose work puts them in front of people during the normal course of business such as bank tellers, customer service representatives, mechanics, cashiers.

People talk, not only about what they buy, but where they bought it and who sold it to them. If you're having an "off" day and allow a bad attitude to anger someone, *you anger 250.*

If the person that you're working with is a "difficult" or irate customer, take the H.E.A. T.

H: Hear them out.   Listen and let them vent.
E: Empathize.   "I can understand."
A: Apologize.   "I'm sorry this happened."
T: Take action.   "Here's what I can do...

Be a pro. Rise above the situation, show your best side you'll bring out the best is others.

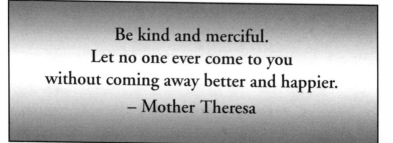

Be kind and merciful.
Let no one ever come to you
without coming away better and happier.
– Mother Theresa

5. "Click" with Your Silent Partner

Every year, 40 of the greatest chefs in the world get together to agree on their favorite restaurant. For ten years in a row, they've consistently named the restaurant owned by legendary Swiss chef, Freddie Girardet. Aside from serving spectacular food, one of the biggest reasons for its continued success is its use of technology.

Every diner is "clicked" into their computer. They record your dining profile—where you sat, what you ate, who prepared your meal, what wines you prefer, and who waited on you. When you return, they're able to greet you by name and review your dining history as a way of building rapport. This small restaurant is world famous for its individual attention and patrons love the highly personalized service. Their silent partner, technology, is what sets them apart.

If you're in business today and not clicking with the incredible power of technology to connect with customers, you're wasting precious sales time. I'm shocked at the number of sales "pros" still at large who aren't using this powerful partner. There are many "contact manager" software packages available for keeping track of virtually every piece of information you could desire, not to mention its research power.

The dictionary defines clicking as "to fit together, to become suddenly clear and intelligible." On the computer, clicking makes your contacts clearer and fits information together in one place for you. Let technology do  the heavy lifting in your business. Get with it and get clicking!

15

6. Stay in Touch

Referrals are terrific but meaningless unless you stay in touch. It doesn't matter if you use a Palm Pilot, a computerized contact manager, or an archaic Rolodex wheel.

A good computerized contact manager allows you to enter in a tremendous amount of information for staying in touch. As you enter the contact name, designate each entry with a filter name such as Customers, Prospects, Ready to Close, Referrals, Friends. This filter allows you to single out one type of group and put the others into the "background" while you work exclusively with that group. If you want to only call contacts you believe will close in half of the sales cycle, the computer will filter out all entries except for those closest to closing.

Stay in touch with your contacts regularly. No one in your file should be left to gather dust. Depending on the contact type, you may want to recontact every 90 to 120 days. Have something of value to share in addition to saying hello--a news item, a new trend in their business, something you've learned. This is a service call. Don't send mixed messages by recommending a new product or service unless you've got something that you genuinely think would be useful. If appropriate, send referrals their way. End without making the person feel that you called to solicit business but rather provide value. The business evolves from the value you give.

Who needs a recall? _____

_____

 *Strive to make "you're welcome" the words you hear most often.*

7. Present Options

If referring sources think that your products or services are too costly for their contacts, they may be reluctant to make a referral in order to avoid putting friends or associates into an embarrassing situation. Anticipate this obstacle and eliminate it before it comes up.

It's possible that your contact only knows one aspect of what you sell—the one he or she bought. Maybe financing options, add-on services, or different models didn't come up that would broaden the field of prospective customers and referrals. You need not go into detail, but at some point mention your other products, services, and options, even if its just highlighted in a brochure.

Let your referral sources know that your goal is to make your product or service available to a broad market. Assure them that you are ready and willing to work with anyone who might have an interest in what you offer.

1. How can you insure that each customer is aware of your other products and/or services?

2. In what ways do you look for opportunities to teach your customers about additional offerings?

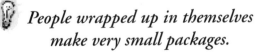

People wrapped up in themselves make very small packages.

8. Be a Leader

In politics those with low seniority, low profile, and little influence are called "back benchers." If you're going to join an organization for networking or any other purpose, be more than a member. Be a leader. Be a leader in your professional associations, organization, or industry.

Run for office. Become president or program chairperson. Be at the front of the room instead of the back. Don't sit on the bench when you can play. Taking a leadership roll greatly increases your professional visibility and with it your exposure to new referral sources.

Here's what leaders do:

1. **Set direction.**
   Effective leaders create a vision of the future and inspire others to share that vision. They also create a mission with a purpose towards fulfilling that vision, enlisting others in the cause. You cannot be a leader less you have followers, and people follow those they believe are worth following. If the vision you're seeking is purposeful (meaningful), principled (ethical), balanced (considers impact in other areas), shared (goes beyond the gain of one individual), and  enduring (has residual value), you've identified a cause worth leading and following.

2. **Be a role model, coach, and helper.**
   Lead by example. Show the way. Be the kind of person you want others to be. Set the bar for excellence by being excellent in all that you do—in character, thought, word, and deed. Also enable others to

participate in your vision and mission by providing resources necessary to get the job done.

3. Provide challenges.

One great aspect of leadership is that you don't have to do all the work. Delegate tasks to others. You'll find that when you empower others to unleash their creativity, everyone benefits. You gain power by giving it away, not hoarding it.

4. Provide rewards and recognition.

The best leaders generously give acknowledgment and appreciation to those who have contributed to the fulfillment of the mission and vision. Recognition for a job well done is the single most powerful motivator. If you're the kind of person who's inclined to say, "Good job," next time say, "Great job." It's free and the benefits that it provides are priceless. People tend to do more of what they're rewarded for. If you want to see people repeat favorable behavior, tell them that you appreciate what they do. Provide formal rewards (i.e. plaques, trophies, pins) or informal rewards such as a simple "Thank you," or "Great job."

List four steps you will take to become a leader:

1.   3.

2.   4.

**Power is about what you can control.
Freedom is about what you can unleash.
– Harriet Rubin**

9. Be Seen and Heard

If you don't have time for a leadership role, at least be seen and heard. When you attend seminars, symposiums, conferences and other types of high visibility events, make it a point to be seen and heard in such a way that will create positive, professional exposure for you. It's free advertising.

When choosing a seat, find a place that makes it easy for others to see and hear you, such as the front left-hand corner of the room. Stand when you speak. Be sure that what you say is interesting, noteworthy, and a constructive contribution. If you play devil's advocate, state that you're playing that role just to be sure all sides are considered. Don't take over the podium or give a lengthy speech though. A few, well-placed remarks—direct and to the point—should be sufficient to make your contribution. If done professionally and intelligently, your comments might serve to stimulate a positive exchange of ideas or gain new insights.

Part of being seen and heard is to act like a host at functions, not a guest. This doesn't mean taking over an agenda or usurping the hosting privilege of those running an event. Hosting means you're in the flow of activities, helping to make the gathering more enjoyable for everyone. Here's the difference between a guest and a host. You decide which one is more effective for building referrals.

Guest	Host
Takes a passive role	Takes an active role
More reserved	More outgoing
Waits to be introduced	Takes initiative
Often feels awkward	Helps others feel relaxed
Waits to be talked to	Initiates conversations

Guest	Host
Waits for invite to activities	Helps host facilitate
Stays in one place	Mingles, makes introductions

Hosting is more easily said than done. We've all had our moments (or hours!) of insecurities in a crowd. You can change all that by preparing your mindset—by not focusing on how nervous you will be, but rather on the enjoyment of meeting new people.

What you pay attention to determines how you feel! If you pay attention to your nerves, you'll be nervous. If you pay attention to the fun of the adventure, you'll have fun. "Act as if" you have a job helping others to feel more secure and you'll feel more secure in the process. It also helps to be prepared before going in. Here are four ways of reducing insecurity so that you can be seen and heard while enjoying yourself:

1. Have conversation starters ready. (See # 28, 69.)

2. Know how to discuss the benefits of your business. (See #28, 34, 43.)

3. Know how to smoothly enter and exit conversations politely. (See #61.)

4. Have questions ready to redirect conversations. (See #61.)

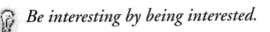 *Be interesting by being interested.*

10. Write an Introductory Letter

Make it easy for your contact to refer you by drafting an introductory letter or postcard that they may send or fax directly to their referral. The purpose of the letter is to outline the general nature of your products or services and how they benefit current customers.

When you give the letter or card to your referring source, mention that you wrote it to help explain what you do, and that you're providing the letter for everyone's convenience. Since you're the expert in what you do, your letter can explain your offerings better than someone less familiar with your business. Your letter should bullet the benefits of what you do. Jot some ideas down here:

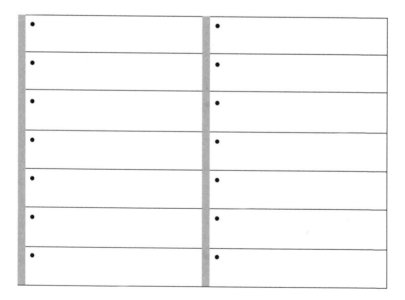

11. Be a Congruent Communicator

Has your conversation ever just clicked with someone? You
understand what the other person is saying without even
exchanging a word.

And you may know the *other* feeling. You try to make a good
connection but everything goes wrong. There are awkward
pauses, you can't think of anything to say, you both start
talking at the same time, then both stop. You begin again but
get interrupted. You try to be helpful and make a suggestion
but the other person thinks you're pushy. You try to be a good
listener, but the other person thinks you're a doormat.

If we could all enjoy clicking with each other, this entry
wouldn't be needed. Although we may think that what we've
said is clear, every conversation is ripe for miscommunication.
If the stakes are low, we might let it pass. But if we're in a
high-stakes situation such as a business meeting, negotiations,
or an interview, what gets said and how it gets said is critical.
Miscommunications can lead to hard feelings, broken relationships and disastrous outcomes. Since so much of referral
building is based on positive relationships, it's critical to learn
how to be a congruent communicator. This means that the
message you *intend* to send is clearly understood.

Every time you communicate, the receiver of your message
will evaluate you on two levels:

1. What is your intended message?

2. What have you taught me about your character?

We form *impressions* by thousand of nonverbal messages that

23

are *pressed* against us. If you want to avoid misunderstandings:

1. Keep your verbal (words), voice, and visual messages all saying the same thing. This is essential if you intend to build credibility, trust., and believability.

2. Be direct, but polite. Avoid hinting or "beating around the bush." Say what you intend to say. The preferred style for business communication is directness. Unfortunately it angers people if it comes on too strong or appears "bossy." Indirect communication however is more tactful, but ripe for miscommunication. Aim for the middle ground that offers the best of both — polite *and* assertive without being aggressive.

   Asian communities advocate indirectness. If you're extremely direct, you can soften your approach by *asking* for what you want, not telling. "How about if we get something to eat?" softens "I want to eat now."

3. Speak in numbers. You might say, "There are three things I'd like to cover." This keeps you and the listener organized on the main points.

4. Write in bullets. It's easier to see the main points of an idea if they're separated from lengthy text with a visual grabber such as a bullet or numbering system.

5. Summarize, paraphrase, or feedback the conversation before adjourning. Repeat your understanding of the message to check for clarity.

If your epitaph etched what you did today, what would your final etching say?"

12. Think "Upside Down"

"Upside Down" thinking is a term used for seeing things from a new angle or a perspective. Instead of looking at what something does, think of what it can't do. Instead of keeping the principles of one area confined to that area, try using them in another area. This new way of looking at the world unleashes your creative juices, helps stimulate innovation, and finds new ways of solving problems for your customers and prospects. First, try these quizzes in order to stimulate your thinking. The great innovators found inspiration from many upside down sources.

Quiz #1
Each innovator below had a childhood toy that became an "energizing principle" for him. Match the genius with his fascination. Then think back: What was your favorite toy? What did you learn from it? How can its lessons help today?

1. Toy rubber-band driven helicopter A. Albert Einstein

2. Magnetic compass   B. R.B. Fuller

3. Explosives   C. Wright brothers

4. Building blocks   D. Samuel Colt

5. Dog   E. Alexander G. Bell

Quiz #2
Try getting your creative juices going with this exercise. By adding only a single line, turn the image below (IX) into a 6:

IX

Answers to Quiz #1

1C — In building their plane, the Wrights were also helped by their skills in building bicycles.

2A — Seeing a compass needle jump toward a magnet made young Einstein yearn to discover "hidden laws," even though teachers declared him dumb. He was in fact, dyslexic.

3D — Colt blew things up for fun. Sent to India to learn discipline, he invented the revolver on his voyage home.

4B — Fuller's light, strong, geodesic dome uses the equilateral triangle as a "building block."

5E — A favorite Bell stunt: making his dog growl, then manipulating his pharynx to say, "How do you do?"

Possible solutions to Quiz #2:

Put a horizontal line through the center, turn it upside down, then cover the bottom to get Roman numeral VI. Or draw an "S" in front of the IX to make SIX. What prevents most people from doing this is that they feel locked into seeing things "one *right* way." The most creative people synthesize known qualities, ideas, and resources in new ways. Discovery means looking at the same thing as everyone else does and thinking something different! In creativity, sometimes to err is to be right!

Here's how upside down thinking helped a phone company promote its service. Instead of asking what a telephone *could* do, it asked the opposite, "What *can't* you do with a phone?" You can't eat a telephone. Then it asked, "Why not?" After challenging this assumption, it came up with chocolate telephones for a national campaign. "Take a bite out of your phone bill with our irresistible service." Sales went up 150% because people talked about the innovative promotion with family and friends.

What innovative solutions will help your prospects?

13. Sail the 5 C's to Success

After meeting people for the first time at social or business gatherings, promptly send them a note expressing how delighted you were to have made their acquaintance.

Personalize your communication as much as possible. A handwritten note is best. In our age of electronic messages, putting a "high touch" to the "high tech" really stands out and says that you value others enough to put in the extra effort.

Include a point of reference in your note by mentioning a part of the conversation that you found interesting, meaningful, or something that you share in common. Now this person is no longer a stranger. Not only have you just made a new friend, you may have just met your new *best* friend.

I call this the 5 C's to Success. Meeting a new contact, showing courtesy and consideration through correspondence, helps to build continued success. Never let past successes allow you to rest. When you rest you rust.

Contact + Courtesy + Consideration + Correspondence = Continued Success

In order to have continual referrals, your goal is to:
- turn suspects into prospects
- turn prospects into customers
- turn customers into clients
- turn clients into friends

Friends buy, refer, and make the business fun.

14. Create a Consistently Credible Public Image

One of the things that can inhibit sources from making referrals is that while they may be pleased with your work, there may be some residual doubt about the consistency of performance. Call it a "sixth" sense, somehow they've created reasonable doubt based on the only thing they have to go on—your public image.

Creating a *consistently* favorable public image means building from the inside out. Character first, appearance second. Turn to the section on ethics (#70) to learn more about character. You can improve character by practicing many of the strategies in this book *simultaneously* - be a professional, be an expert, get published, lead worthwhile causes, be honest, help others to help themselves, and walk your talk.

Go through the checklist at the beginning of this book. Check off all the ideas that will build your image and set goals to implement each one. This will ensure that you're employing all of the strategies at your disposal to create a consistently credible public image and build your referral business.

Then go to work on how you *physically* present yourself to others. This will depend on the nature of your work. You may wish to network to find an image consultant, (the better department stores have free personal shopper services), to sand off any rough edges. For those needing a professional wardrobe, here are some helpful hints from clothing and wardward expert, John Malloy:

1. Basic Professional Woman's Wardrobe

- ◆ black, navy, or grey skirt suit
- ◆ navy and black belt
- ◆ good quality, conservative watch
- ◆ three coordinated skirts and jackets
- ◆ black, navy, and taupe flats or pumps
- ◆ three solid-colored blouses or silk "shells"
- ◆ complimentary scarf
- ◆ two pastel blouses
- ◆ all-purpose knee-length coat
- ◆ black, brown, or burgundy briefcase
- ◆ good quality jewelry—gold or silver
- ◆ conservative black, brown, or navy handbag

2. Basic Professional Men's Wardrobe

- ◆ all clothing clean, pressed, lint and spot-free
- ◆ polished, and "soulful" shoes
- ◆ buttons in place
- ◆ buttoned, double breasted jackets when standing
- ◆ one charcoal grey suit
- ◆ one navy suit
- ◆ one medium blue or grey suit
- ◆ one pair black leather lace-up shoes
- ◆ one pair slip on shoes
- ◆ blue or pin-striped shirt
- ◆ good quality watch
- ◆ all-purpose knee-length coat
- ◆ black or brown leather briefcase
- ◆ 2 black leather belts
- ◆ 6-8 solid striped or patterned silk tie
- ◆ six white long sleeved cotton shirts

What do you need to do to sharpen up your public image?

15. Leverage Yourself: Speak UP!

The great mathematician Archimedes once said, "Give me a lever long enough and I can lift the world." One of the most powerful ways to build referrals is through the principle of leverage--with the right tool you can maximize your results with the least amount of effort. This means that instead of meeting one person at a time, you can meet dozens, hundreds, or even thousands all at once. One way you can effectively leverage your time is through public speaking. Before you panic and flip to the next entry, take a moment to look at what leveraging yourself can do to help more people.

First, let's address the hard part—speaking in front of groups. I used to think that public speaking was one of the greatest *unthinkable* thoughts—cannibalism, incest, public speaking. I'm not alone in my terror. According to the *Book of Lists,* public speaking is the #1 fear of most people. Death is #7. People would rather die than talk in front of people.

But fear of public speaking is like any other fear – it's False Evidence Appearing Real. We manufacture our fears. One person's fear is another's adventure. Every time you speak to someone, you're speaking in public! The problem sets in when the group gets larger. Being rejected by one person is bad enough, but we'd rather have root canal than be rejected by an entire group!

Most everyone, especially great speakers, were fearful of public speaking at first. The people who overcome their fear simply stick with it. If you do it often enough, the fear disappears as you relax into what you're there to do—provide value to others. The focus should not be on *you* (how am I doing?), but on the message and benefits you bring to others.

> ### *It's not about you, it's about them!*

Here's how to get started. Put your fears aside and write an outline for a 30-45 minute talk that consists of three main points and supporting material for each point--5-10 minutes per point, no more than three or four points per program.

Add some visuals such as overheads, slides, posters, a video clip, a flip chart illustration, or if you're computer savvy—a PowerPoint presentation to reinforce your points. Even better, try to make your program interactive by involving the audience in discussions or a workshop exercise. When you ask others to be part of your program, it makes developing your program easier and people remember what they see and do.

The important part of your talk is your opening and closing. You may start by:
- Asking a compelling, relevant question
- Ask the audience to do something
- Relate a relevant incident
- Use a relevant magic trick
- Make a relevant visual demonstration
- Pay a genuine compliment
- Tell a relevant story
- Use a relevant humorous joke
- Quote from a well-known source
- Reveal a shocking statistic

When you close, end with a call to action.
- Present a challenge
- Use a motivating quotation or story
- Hammer home the benefits to the audience for taking action
- Present a compelling, convincing summary

31

After your opening, use the 3 T's.

1. Tell them what you're going to tell them.
2. Tell them.
3. Tell them what you told them.

Don't make your talk a commercial for your products or services. Your information will be what attracts people to you.

Next, call the "chair people" of local organizations such as Rotary Club, Optimists, and Lions. Your Chamber of Commerce generally has listings of your local service clubs. These folks have regular meetings and are constantly on the lookout for those who can provide a valuable program to their members. Explain what the members will gain from your talk and ask to be scheduled as the guest speaker. Also ask what their protocol is for distributing brochures and promotional materials. Most allow the distribution of take-home material on a back table or at each place setting.

At the end of your program, conduct a raffle. Ask everyone to take out a business card and write the word "Yes" on it if they would like to be contacted for a free "something," an estimate, consultation, or whatever's appropriate with your line of work. Then collect the cards, have an audience member pull one out and give away something of value—a book, tape, plaque, gift basket, or part of your services/product.

Later you'll be presenting at your professional association. Your credibility and referrals will soar. Toastmasters International provides a supportive environment in which to hone your public speaking skillswww.toastmasters.org/

The challenges before you are the stepping stones of your rewards.

16. Plant Seeds of Suggestions

Plant seeds of suggestion by mentioning to your contacts how fortunate you are to have people referring business your way. Let them know that you've built your business by word of mouth or "work of mouth." Explain what a genuine honor it is for you to have satisfied customers (or clients) telling friends and acquaintances how they have benefited from your product or service. This helps others to feel comfortable in making a referral when the appropriate time comes.

Planting seeds of suggestions is just that—a subtle reference to the idea of referrals, especially with non-business contacts. Use a "By the way…" indirect approach to avoid appearing pushy or desperate. This technique not only helps develops contacts from friendships, but friendships from contacts.

Write how you will indirectly mention that your business is built on referrals:

_____

_____

_____

_____

> **My green thumb came only as a result of the mistakes I made while learning to see things from the plant's point of view.**
> **– H. Fred Ale**

33

17. Partner

Many businesses are entering into partnering relationships with other businesses. These are often formed between people in related fields, but partnering with the competition has great value as well.

Consider a strategic alliance or joint venture with another organization. A formal arrangement may be to develop technology with another company, or a simple venture may be to coadvertise a product or service. These relationships can give you access to capital, international markets, new distribution channels, new technology, credibility, and reduced costs.

Set up partnerships that have reciprocal value:
- stock brokers and accountants
- hotels and car rentals
- airlines and hotels
- greeting card retailers and florists
- Realtors/lenders/escrow/title
- free-lance writers and graphic artists

I met the top producing stock broker at a major investment firm who said he had more business than he could handle from his partnership with an accountant. Both referred business to each other when they uncovered a client need that the other could provide. He interviewed many accountants to get the right fit. By giving, he became a wealthy order taker.

Competing automobile dealerships and restaurants partner with each other by locating themselves on the same block and sharing advertising expenses, drawing customers for all. With whom can you partner?

18. Reward Referrals

One of the greatest business secrets is:

> ## The rewarded customer buys, refers, and returns.

When you reward a customer for a referral, that customer will reward you with repeat business and more referrals. A reward is anything you give your customers or contacts that conveys the message: *Thank you. I appreciate your referrals.*

Here's a list of reward suggestions:

1. a handwritten thank you note
2. phone call and thank you
3. flowers
4. gift basket
5. balloons
6. candy
7. merchandise or gift certificate
8. personalized items
9. dinner for two
10. a finder's fee (if appropriate)

Ali Lassen of the Leads Club writes in her Power Plays booklet about a woman whose trademark Thank-You note is a new one dollar bill placed inside a plain card with a her hand written message that says, "Your referral is worth a million of these to me!" By handwriting the card, she not only saves on the price of an average store-bought card ($1.50), but can also change the word, "referral" to lead, business, or recommendation to reflect the circumstance of her gratitude. Her clients are always "warmed" when thanked with cold cash.

The National Institute of Business Management says that a gift should be given when you'd like to acknowledge appreciation of a business acquaintance who's been thoughtful, i.e. referred business your way. It recommends that the gift not be used as a *direct* response to the receipt of an order. This will look more like a bribe, even though your intentions are pure.

If kept in a range of $25 - $50, your gift will provide an appropriate message without appearing to bribe your customer or client for more business. A gift from one CEO to another might range from $50 - $100. A note should accompany the gift, but it shouldn't specifically refer to business or thank the recipient for business. Generally large ticket sales may be accompanied by a gift as a gesture of thanks after the business has been concluded. A general gift thank you card might read, "It was a pleasure working with you."

If you send a gift to someone as a means of saying thank you for a referral, be sure to be consistent in your gift giving. Each time someone sends a referral your way, send that person a similar reward. For instance, if you sent a thank you note for the first referral, continue to send thank you notes. If you sent a $25 gift, continue to send items in that price range. Sending consistent rewards eliminates confusing messages to your referral source.

Who would you like to reward for referrals?

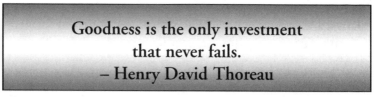

Goodness is the only investment
that never fails.
– Henry David Thoreau

19. Offer Incentives

Incentives are different from rewards in that they take place before the sale, rewards take place after the sale.

One grocery store's slogan is, "Tell a Friend." When you tell your friends to shop at their store, you're asked to give the friend a membership card into their discount club with your name and membership number on it. When the card gets turned in, you're given automatic discounts off your purchases at the register. It's one way the store tells their customers, "Thank you. We value your business."

When offering an incentive, never make your customers act against their will, feel intimidated, or bribed. It must be presented as a way for you to thank them for their continued business. You might say, "I value your business. To show my appreciation, I'd like to give you and the next person you refer a 10% discount."

If not properly presented, incentives can promote greed. A customer may give you names of inappropriate prospects just to collect the gift. You end up with names, but no qualified prospects. This could end up adversely affecting your customer relationship as you come to resent or mistrust his or her judgment. It could also cost you referrals that would have come through other strategies mentioned in this book.

Incentives work, as in the case of the grocery store. Just be careful how you administer them.

 Words can comfort and words can teach, but in the end it's action that speaks.

37

20. Ask Customers

The fastest way to obtain referrals is to ask for them. You can ask *anyone* you know, but your strongest leads will come from customers immediately after a sale. Buying enthusiasm is the highest then because they're pleased with their purchase and pleased with you for helping. When you're given names, get as much information as possible about the lead:

1. name and company name (if appropriate)
2. phone number and email
3. relationship to the referral source
4. pertinent background information

Be sure to ask for permission to use the customer's name.

In big-ticket sales, your customers might be reluctant to refer you until they've had time to verify the performance of your product/service. Call 15 days after the sale to follow through, then 2 weeks later for referrals. You might say:

> "I'm so pleased that we were able to help you with what you needed. This is what makes our work so worthwhile. By the way, who else do you think would be interested in (name the *benefits* of your product or service)? I'd like to let them know what's available and help them out as well."

Most people won't have names on the tip of their tongues. Narrow their field of vision by naming groups such as:

- business associates
- friends
- church members
- social groups
- neighbors
- hobbyists/sports connections
- relatives
- clubs
- professional groups
- acquaintances

After you've been given the leads and contact information, and their relationship to your customer, ask:

> "I'd be happy to give them a call, or would you prefer getting in touch with them first just to let them know I'll be calling?"

> If they prefer to contact their referral first, then ask for a re-contact period such as,

> "Would you like me to call you back tomorrow, or would two days be enough time for you to make contact?"

Offer a choice, letting them know that you'll be calling them back. This keeps the spirit of the referrals active while bringing closure to the introductory calls.

Write down the names as soon as your customer (or referring source) provides them, and be sure to get contact numbers (email addresses etc.) so that you don't have to go back to your customer and begin the process over again.

Some sales people become overly aggressive asking for referrals, especially if they haven't made a sale and want to justify the time they've spent with a prospect. This strong-arm pressure approach may yield results, but inevitably it catches up with the aggressor. If someone resents how you're asking or regrets giving you a referral, he or she may call the referred contact and warn them not to buy from you, even though they may be pleased with the product or service.

To whom have you provided superior service and can call on for referrals?

21. Ask Prospects

Anyone who's been in sales for a day quickly learns that not every prospect shares your enthusiasm for what you do. It's frustrating to hear the word "No" when you truely believe that your product or service will help others solve problems.

To deal with the frequency of rejection, some sales managers train their reps to think in terms of closing averages. If it takes an average of 20 prospect contacts to close a sale, reps are trained to think, "Thank you for your rejection Mr. Prospect. I am one contact closer to the 20th call and making a sale."

While there's nothing wrong with this psychology, you can maximize prospecting time and increase the value of each contact by asking for referrals, even though the person you're talking to may not be interested in buying. Asking a prospect might sound like this:

> "I understand that this isn't a fit for you, but who else do you know that might be interested in... (name the *benefit** of your product or service)?"

*Benefits are the end solutions to problems, not the features or means to the end. Benefits are how your products or services help people save time, lower costs, increase convenience, improve quality, and/or build security.

 When a prospect says "No" when you ask for an appointment or the order, you're in the red zone of selling. If you're unable to resolve your prospect's concerns, you have nothing to lose by asking for the names of others who may benefit from what you do. This technique works only if your earnestness to help others is genuine.

When we moved to California many years ago, a realtor tried to help us find a home. We couldn't find one in the limited time we had so we wound up renting a friend's home. Even though we were unsuccessful in buying from Marcia, she had so thoroughly impressed us with her ethics, knowledge of the market, genuine caring, and *sound advice* that we became loyal advocates. (See #16—it works!)

"I know you weren't able to buy now," she said, "but if you ever decide to buy a home in the future or know of someone who's looking to buy or sell, please give me a call." She didn't get a commission for her time. In fact there were two houses we wanted that she advised against so she lost money with us.

When our friend returned a year later, he decided to put the house we were renting from him on the market. In spite of its amenities, we called Marcia to see what else was available.

She said, "I know the inventory andthere's not much out there. I'd love to show you around and I'd love the commission, but my advice is to buy the house you're in." Twice she sacrificed making a sale in order to give us her best advice.

We bought our friend's house and happily lived there for another 17 years. We were never able to buy from her, but over the years we referred many friends and acquaintances because we trusted her judgement. Each time she sold a home through one of our referrals, she sent a beautiful gift basket. Even though we were never able to be her customer, she earned our referrals through her advice, honesty, and because she asked!

You can help others by helping yourself.
Ask for what you need in order to serve others.

41

22. Prospect Your Own Backyard

If your company has a service and/or parts department for maintenance and repairs of the product you sell, this is a prime source of referrals, especially for electronic or mechanical products. When repairs start to add up, the owner may be ready for a trade-in, upgrade, or a new model.

Keep a frequent and consistent dialogue going with your service department to learn who's been in for repairs. Either make yourself part of the service call or make contact after the estimate is in. This is an excellent opportunity to provide customers with an escape from costly repairs.

Don't act like a "vulture" however when recommending a trade-in. If it's not done with the spirit of genuine caring, it can easily look like an ambush. Make sure that you can make a reasonable case to your customer that buying beats the cost of repairing. If you can't, don't try. Instead, do the next best thing. Give your customer a long range prognosis as to when repairing the product will cease to be cost effective and either make a tickler note for a recall or set up an appointment to discuss a new purchase at that time.

When customers perceive that you're attentive to their needs, they will naturally speak favorably of you to others.

What's your next step for prospecting your backyard?

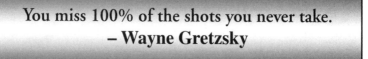

You miss 100% of the shots you never take.
– Wayne Gretzsky

23. Work the Itch Cycle

An "itch cycle" is the average length of time it takes for a product or service to wear out its usefulness. When it becomes inadequate, obsolete, too costly to maintain, or even boring, customers think about buying again.

Some products or services have built in obsolescence or need frequent renewal. Software is in perpetual improvement, so users upgrade every six months to a year. People needing accountants have an annual itch cycle every January to April. Home buyers move an average of every 5-10 years. People think about trading in their automobile about every two and half years. Office equipment is cycled about every three years. Your product or service's itch cycle is determined by the length of time it takes to mature into obsolescence.

You can determine your itch cycle with a market survey of your company's past customers' average buying cycles.

1. Go through your files and call past customers. Ask how they're enjoying their product or service and how long they've used it. Find out how many times they've bought since their original purchase. (Don't count onetime buyers or extremes. You want average cycles.)

2. After you've collected at least twenty numbers, add them together and divide by the number of entries you're counting to find the norm of your itch cycle.

Contact your past customers and clients about 60 days before the itchiest time. Staying on top of buying cycles not only provides exceptional service, but builds relationships that build your business.

43

24. Time Your Test Periods

Sometimes customers want to see how well your product or service delivers on its promise before referring you to others. In this case, either ask your customers when they'd like to be recontacted in order to get their feedback, or recommend a time that you think allows for a sufficient test period.

If your product or service requires after-sale follow-through visits (for training, installation, maintenance), ask your customer if they've told anyone else about their purchase. People often mention their purchases to friends or associates because of their genuine excitement, to make small talk, or even to boast a little. Ask how their friends reacted to the news. If the response was favorable, ask if they think their friend or associate may be interested in owning or having similar benefits with your product or service. If you detect a green light, your customer may give you the name of the person to call or call ahead for you. This will pave the way for your phone call and possibly new business.

If your product or service doesn't require an after sales call, ask your customer if they *intend* to tell anyone. Find out their motives through friendly conversational questions. Ask if they believe that person might be interested in something similar. If you detect a green light, let your customer know that you'd be happy to help them as well. Get the name and number of the referral. Ask your customer if they would be willing to pass your name along, or let them know that you'd be happy to contact the referral directly to save them the time. Be sure to ask for permission to use their name.

We are what we repeatedly do.
Excellence is not an act but a habit.

25. Adopt an Orphan

When sales professionals leave a company, they also often leave an unsupervised book of business or accounts called "orphans." These abandoned customers can be a gold mine for anyone willing to take on new clients. If your company has territory protection, you'll have to work within that policy. If not, don't ignore this rich source of new business.

Research abandoned files to find unsupervised accounts or one-time customers. Call ahead to update the contact information. Is the person who purchased the product or service still at that location and in a buying position?

These files are pre-qualified leads because they represent people who've already bought and have an interest in what you provide. There's good reason to believe that these customers will be happy to talk to you again. Call and set up a time to introduce yourself and become acquainted with their current needs.

Determine the itch cycle (see #23) and recontact orphans 60 days in advance. If your product or service lends itself to a drop-in visit, you'll save everyone time. (It's also more difficult to ignore a live person waiting in the lobby.) Making an in-person courtesy visit allows you to reintroduce yourself as the one who's assigned to the territory. It's rare that courtesy calls are turned away. Being polite brings out politeness in others.

What is your next step for adopting orphans?

26. Market With Your Customers

I once worked with a company that openly enlisted customers in their marketing strategy. At the end of each sale, representatives told customers that they were able to keep fees low because they worked on straight referrals. Since no money was invested in advertising, they passed those savings along to clients. Then they asked customers if they wanted to help keep fees low and to become part of the marketing plan. Customers eagerly gave them lists of contacts to call.

You can use the same technique. Ask your customers if they would like to help you keep rates down. When you hear a "Yes," ask if they know of anyone who might be interested in your offering. Not only will you be able to help their friends and associates, but you'll also be able to cut back on advertizing and pass those savings along to your clients.

This request should be positioned as a cooperative effort. If everyone enters into it with the intention of helping everyone else profit, it can be very effective. As with any referral you ask for, keep the pressure low-key. The spirit of this tool is for mutual benefit.

Enlisting your customers in your marketing plan is even easier if they ask how you manage to keep your prices low. Your customers have literally opened the door for you to explain your marketing strategy and ask if they'd like to contribute by supplying referrals. Everyone gains with this technique.

The people who need help the most are the ones most likely not to know it.

27. Get Published

Having your words in print is one of the most powerful ways to build your credibility and "celebrity" status. As your standing in the community grows, so will your referrals. People are eager to recommend those who not only offer a valued product or service, but have become a respected authority on it as well.

You can start small by writing letters to editors of your local papers, then move up to larger articles on your area of expertise. You can contribute to trade publications, magazines, newsletters, or any other written media. You can also write a book or a booklet.

It's been said that almost everyone has at least one good book inside, just waiting to be written. If you're an expert in your field, set time aside each day to write that book. You have three alternatives with publishing: 1) publishing houses, 2) self-publishing with distribution channels, or 3) "vanity press" in which you pay for the entire publishing project and distribution yourself. Each has advantages and drawbacks.

Many successful business people have earned the reputation of being experts by writing small pamphlets and giving them to prospects and clients. There's no need to be stuck at the roadblock of big-time publishing. Many people are making their name by self-publishing their own works. New technologies such as desktop publishing and print on demand make it possible. Check out www.iuniverse.com. They will print and distribute, paying you a 20% royalty for as little as $99.

Another approach to being published is to read publications and respond to items about which you feel strongly. Interpret general information; write about its significance or impact to your area of expertise. Analyze and interpret the statements, activities, or newsworthy items of well-known businesses, political, or economic leaders. Then write press releases or letters to the editor of various publications that might be interested in your opinion. Or try publishing an e-newsletter. Over a period of time, people will come to recognize your name. You may even be asked to write a regular column if you develop a following.

It all sounds great you say, but you can't write—just plain and simply cannot write—never could, never will. In that case, hire a ghostwriter. That's what they're there for— to put your ideas on paper for you. The costs of hiring a writer will be inconsequential compared to the returns on how your increased visibility and credibility grow your business.

Many of your clients are in the same position you're in. They need to market their business just as you do. Facilitate this mutual need by suggesting joint publishing such as co-authoring an article or news column. It could be about how you both solved an industry problem or industry trends.

Offer to write the article for your customer to save time. Work together on an outline, write the piece, then ask for editorial input from your customer. Put both of your names on the finished piece. Your customer now has a vested interested in distributing it to his or her circle of influence. When others see that your customer respects your work enough to co-author an article, your referrals will increase dramatically.

 Every job is a self-portrait of who you are.
Autograph your work with excellence.

28. Initiate Conversations

Whenever you're with people, especially at a networking event, you'll feel more comfortable if you know how to make introductions and start conversations.

1. How to Introduce Your Boss:

a. Begin by saying your boss's name first. If you know the other person's name, say it as well. Mention the department, title, or appropriate information (neutral or positive) about the person as a conversation starter.

Bill, I'd like you to meet Carol Carter. Carol this is my new manager Bill Gatlin. He's just joined us from Microlink. We think he'll be a terrific team addition.

b. When in doubt, don't use first names.

c. If someone forgets to introduce you, take the initiative. State your name, company, and ask about the other person's line of work. Show an interest in learning about others first. If they ask about your work, have a 10 second "commercial" ready that explains the benefits of what you do (see #43).

I don't believe we've met. I'm _____ from _____. And you are?.....

What type of work are you in? How did you get started?

What interested you in this type of work?

49

2. How to approach an introduction:

a. Stand up.

b. Walk towards the other person with a smile and steady eye contact.

c. Extend your hand and shake hands. (Part your fingers slightly and you will make better contact.)

d. Introduce yourself. After hearing the other person's name, repeat it: "It's a pleasure to meet you Bob."

3. Behavior Checklist for Conversations

When you talk with others, do you: (Yes/No)

Y	N	
		a. smile genuinely as appropriate
		b. use open body language (no crossed arms)
		c. use an engaging voice (not over-bearing or monotone)
		d. have occasional nods of understanding
		e. use good steady eye contact, about 3-5 seconds before looking away
		f. avoid looking at "outside" distractions i.e other people talking (If necessary, walk your guest to a more quiet location.)
		g. use a slight forward lean to show interest

29. Become an Expert

You have it within your power to not only be *known* as an expert, but actually *become* an expert. If you invest 30 minutes a day reading in your chosen field, at the end of one year you will be an expert in that area. When you write and give presentations on what you've learned, others will come to see you as an expert resource.

Devote 30 minutes each day researching information that others will find beneficial. You can simply summarize and present data gathered by others to your clients, or create new information through surveys or questionnaires on such things as trends, buying behavior, or consumer tastes.

Writing articles, pamphlets, newsletters, and books is a great way to build your credibility and expertise (see #27). The important thing is to identify yourself as your industry's "go-to" person. When this happens prospects will seek you out.

If you have something timely and interesting to offer the media they'll be interested. It's their job to find new material. In exchange, you'll receive free coverage and publicity. Be professional when contacting media with your news releases. Follow up with an appropriate phone call, but don't pester. Respect their time and deadlines. They get many requests.

When you become known as an expert in your field, newspaper, radio, and TV will be seeking you out as an expert authority to help them tell their stories. You'll be seen as a valuable *on-going* resource. Your goal is to become part of their stable of contacts. Whenever they need an expert in your field to interpret events, you'll be the one they call.

30. Exceed the Four Levels of Customer Expectations

The Gallup Poll's twenty-year study of over one billion customers revealed four levels of customer expectations:

1. Accuracy – People expect what they buy to be accurate. If you order lasagna, you expect lasagna. You expect your bills to be correct, all the parts to be in the box, or the size to meet specifications.

2. Availability – Do you have ample parking, 800 lines, 24-hour help service, extended hours? Are you there when customers need you?

These first two levels are easily solved with technology and are therefore easy for competitors to copy. Providing them does not create satisfied customers, but merely prevents dissatisfaction and complaints.

3. Partnering – This level engages the creative side of solving customer problems. It means you empathize with customers' unique situations and seek mutually beneficial solutions. (See #17.)

4. Advice – You are the expert. Help guide customer decisions. When you're able to teach customers about what to do, learning leads to loyalty and customer advocacy.

Levels three and four turn prospects into fans who sing your praises. It's free advertising and a tremendous boost for building referrals.

31. Be a Teacher

Sometimes you'll run into people who not only don't know about the value of referrals, but also how the referral process works. These people may have benefited from referrals in the past, may even have made referrals, but for some reason they just don't recognize the importance of *consistency!*

When you run into this situation, it may be time to put on your educator's cap. If you've concluded that your contact doesn't know about the referral side of business, teach him! See this as your opportunity to mentor, from one business professional to another, providing value-added learning. Remember that learning leads to loyalty and customer advocacy (see #16)—meeting the highest levels of customer expectations. If you can help others to help themselves, you'll create customers for life.

Begin by telling your business customer or client how consistent referrals have helped build your business, then explain how it works. Urge them to always be on the lookout for referral possibilities. You may even want to give them this book as a gift. It's up to you to teach them that when the wheels of referrals are spinning at peak capacity, sales soar.

Throughout this process, maintain the role of teacher with the spirit of educating, not doing business. If you take care to teach well, the business will take care of you.

The more we expect, the less we accept.
Don't let the tyranny of rising expectations
get you down.

53

32. Rank Your Referrals

Anyone can be a source of referrals, but some will be more prolific than others. Practice good time management by working with those that bring in 80% of your referrals.

You may find it useful to categorize your lead sources into priority groupings. Make up an A list of your "hottest" and most prolific referral sources. Your B, C, and even a D list would categorize other sources by their descending order of frequency of referral. Setting up partnerships (see #17) can get this revolving door of steady referrals going.

People of influence or authority generally have more contacts. These might be association committee members, executives, editors, publishers, or civic leaders. These high producers are the "seeds" in your garden of contacts who can broadcast your worth to many others in a short period of time through their newsletters, promotional pieces, or from the simple fact that they're in front of a lot of people.

If you ever need to cut back on your business due to family obligations, illness, or added responsibilities, ration your attention using the 80-20 rule of sales. Eighty percent of your business will come from 20% of your client base. The same thing applies to referrals: 80% of your referrals will come from 20% of your contacts. Know who the key players are and work to keep your name in front of them.

 *There is no traffic jam on the extra mile.*

33. Volunteer

Becoming known in your community for your volunteer work is a worthy undertaking in and of itself, regardless of your business needs. But the fact that you can increase your circle of influence and pool of contacts makes it a good way to leverage your time to serve more people.

Churches, local papers, and your Chamber of Commerce are three resources for learning about volunteer possibilities in your community. Find something that matches your talents or interests. Go in with your heart, not your head.

Please don't view this act of generosity as anything other than that--a way to give back. As with so many of these suggestions, tactfulness goes a long way. Don't use this as a way to exploit that cause for your own benefit.

When you start to do volunteer work, keep your eyes on the bigger issue, not the size of your contact files. If you work side by side with others in trying to solve a problem or make community improvements, others will add to your contacts without being asked.

What volunteer work would give you an opportunity to utilize your talents for the good of others?

One of the most beautiful compensations of this life is that no one can sincerely try to help another without helping himself.
– Ralph Waldo Emerson

34. Brand Yourself

While products and services are typically branded, it's just as important for business professionals to brand themselves with a unique identity. It builds customer loyalty and referrals by building name recognition.

Self-branding takes many forms. It can be as simple as creating a unique business card or as elaborate as sponsoring a float in the local founders' day parade. The point is that it has to contribute in a positive way to your professional identity.

One title insurance representative branded herself with realtors using the image of sneakers. She wanted to differentiate herself with speed (see #2), so she wore colorful sneakers, put a picture of sneakers on her business card, and added a brand that read, "When speed counts you can count on me." While other reps also delivered on speed, she became the top producing title rep simply because she branded her image.

To brand yourself, ask yourself questions such as:
1. What unique benefits do your product or services offer your potential customers?
2. What is your USP (Unique Selling Proposition)? How are you different? If you're in a commodity market, it's essential that you differentiate yourself.
3. Does your promotional material convey your personal and/or professional uniqueness?
4. Are there things you can do "outside the box" of sales that will enhance your identity?

What will be your unique "branded" identity?

35. Be a Card Carrier

How to Present Your Business Cards:
When you're attending a network gathering, wear clothing with pockets so that you can get to your cards quickly without fumbling. Bring about 30 cards with you and keep them in your left pocket for easy access. Keep a pen in another pocket for making notes on the cards.

At an appropriate moment in the conversation, you might begin with, "I'd like one of your cards to keep on file in case I'm ever asked for the name of someone in your line of work. Here's one of mine so we can stay in touch." Place the cards you receive in your right pocket so that you can stay organized. You might also say, "Let me give you one of my cards. I'd love to stay in touch. May I have one of yours?"

After you've left the conversation, make notes you'd like to remember on the back of the card such as, "Just had a baby. Send a card." Or, "Set up conference call," or " Likes golf and plays the trumpet." Contact information and notes should be transferred to your contact manager so that all your information is organized in one place. Prompt your file to "tell" you any follow-through action items that need to be taken.

Cards are important, but not everyone carries them today. You're just as likely to get an email or a web address scribbled on a napkin. And all too often people who normally carry cards, run out before they can replenish their supply.

When you meet someone without a business card—don't let that stop business from happening. Have an information request card handy. An information request card is a small postcard with your name, address, and contact information printed on one side. The reverse side asks recipients to fill in information:

- Name
- Title
- Company name
- Address
- Phone number
- Email
- Request:
  - Call me
  - Send literature
  - Set up appointment
  - Other _____

Offering an information request card is not only a great way to elicit feedback from potential customers, but it also saves you both from embarrassment if exchanging business cards looks like it's going to be a one-way street.

This is also one of those professional touches that will set you apart from the average. It sends the subliminal message that a great many people are asking for your material — so much so that you've had to prepare special request cards!

> **Grant that we may not so much seek to be understood as to understand.**
> **– St. Francis of Assisi**

36. Cultivate Current Clients

Your existing clients and customers are an excellent resource for obtaining referrals and repeat business. These are your strongest connections because your ongoing interaction with them keeps you fresh in their minds and excited about what you do.

Invest time each month marketing to your past and current clients. You'd be amazed at how much repeat business and referrals you can achieve when you recontact current clients. This is an excellent opportunity to upsell. Let them know about your current projects without implying that you're in need of work. A newsletter or email does this effectively as well. Let them know about additional products and services.

The best time to make this contact is when there's been some positive change in your product or service or when you have new promotional material available. I contact my speaker bureaus four times a year with quarterly updates in a direct mailing. When special situations don't present themselves often enough, remind your customers of what it was that inspired them do business with you in the first place—service, cost, selection, convenience, inventory--whatever. Everyone can use a review now and then, even loyal customers.

What current client can you call to upsell?

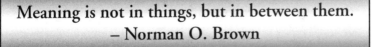

Meaning is not in things, but in between them.
– Norman O. Brown

37. Be an MVP

In sports an MVP is a Most Valuable Player. In the world of sales though, an MVP is a Most Valuable Prospector.

An MVP is not someone who prospects night and day in order to make more sales, but rather one who finds out *what prospects value* and sells to those values. MVPs begin by asking value-driven questions that might sound like this:

> "What's most important in…" such as,
> "What's most important in the home you're looking for, your financial security, the copies you make, the vehicle's performance?"
>
> "What's on your wish list, in order of importance?"
>
> "What would the ideal situation be?"

Unless you ask for your prospect's values, you're prejudging. You can try to guess or "pitch" your products or services, but it's like throwing mud at a wall. Some will stick but most will wind up on the floor. Find out explicit values (obvious) and implicit (hidden) by asking questions. For example, when I sold advertising and business owners said to me, "The ad costs too much," I knew money was tight. I would reply, "So what you're saying is that money is an issue and that you'd like to find a way to be more profitable? The way to do that is to bring in more customers. Here's how we can make this happen…" The ad would pay for itself by bringing in one sale.

> **Your playing small does not serve the world.**
> **– Marianne Williamson**

38. Network

Networking is one of the most powerful strategies for building referrals. It simply means interacting with others for
mutual assistance or support. The best networkers are socially
involved, people oriented, and active members of a professional or community group. Here are some of the benefits
you'll gain from networking:

1. increased flow of referrals
2. reciprocity: helping others while they help you
3. more resources at your disposal
4. opportunities to solve more problems for others
5. increased visibility
6. more friends and fun in the business

If you don't have a strong network, you're probably working
too hard. Contrary to what some believe, when it's done
"right," it's not manipulative nor does it exploit others. It
simply creates an enormous pool of resources, talents, and
experience to draw upon for *everyone*. It also introduces you
to knowledgeable, worthwhile allies that can help you navi-
gate the challenges of your business.

Effective networking means following the Golden Rule of
Business:

Do for others what you'd like to have done for you.

Effective networking isn't a 9-5 enterprise. Hardly an hour of
the day goes by that doesn't present a networking opportunity.
Here are examples:

61

- Professional   Groups   and   Associations
- Industry Special Project Groups
- Non-Profit Organizations
- Political Parties
- Recreational Groups
- Civic Organizations
- Cultural Activities
- Volunteer Work
- Your Christmas Card/Address List
- Educational Institutions
- Chamber of Commerce
- Employee Activities
- Sports Groups
- College/University Courses
- Alumni Organizations
- Toastmasters
- Junior League
- Girl and Boy Scouts
- PTA
- Local Retail Stores
- Special Community Events
- Local Gym/Workout Clubs
- Parenting Groups
- Day Care
- Chat Rooms (on the web)
- Charity Work
- Company Groups or Special Events
- Company Committees i.e. projects, picnics, teams
- Other:

It's possible to spend a lot of money on networking, so consider your affiliations carefully. Find out the difference between groups that organize mixers, 'tip clubs,' and true referral organizations by asking the membership chairpeople. Cheaper is not always better. Check out your Chamber of Commerce for a listing in your community.

1. List all of the networking groups you're part of or intend to join in the next three months. It's better to limit your involvement and do it well rather than spread yourself too thin and end up with poor results.

2. What groups do you plan to call or network this month? This week?

3. Call and ask if you may attend as a visitor or go with a friend. Call the membership chairperson and ask for the protocol on attendance.

4. Write the date of the event on your calendar and go!

5. Follow through on commitments and enter new contacts in your database/contact manager.

If you're not sure where to put your time and attention, choose the one group that suit your needs and interests most. Some groups do not involve joining, just attendance. A blend of both means you can network without becoming overextended. Here is a list of criteria to help you choose your networking groups:

1. Choose groups that interest you at a personal/fulfillment level. If you care about the purpose of the group, you'll get better results, not the least of which is personal satisfaction. Be proud to be a member.

2. Visit the groups you're considering two times before

committing. Most allow at least one free visit.

- Find out from some of the members why they joined and the benefits of membership.

- What are your obligations as a member?

- If it's a hard-core networking group you'd like to join, find out from some of the members how much business they've generated as a result of joining.

- Find out who's on the membership roster. If there are many others in your line of work, you may want to consider joining another group.

- Don't join unless you're going to be an active participant for at least six months.

If you regulate your people orientation like a light switch—on and off—your ability to benefit from networking will be severely compromised. Everyone needs alone time to recharge their batteries, but once you've recharged, get back out there and *be* there 100%. If you waste even 1/2 hour a day not making some kind of connection, be it email, phone, mail, or face-to-face, by the end of the year you will have lost the month of February! Over time, that productivity loss could amount to hundreds of thousands of dollars. For your networking efforts to be effective:

- Connect with people in casual conversation wherever you go (stores, church, errands, elevators).

- Show an interest in learning about others first.

- Help others achieve their goals first. Doing so will

inspire others to help you.

Guidelines for attending a formal networking function:

- Set networking goals before going in. Leave with at least two or three new contacts. With whom do you want to meet or reconnect? Keep your business cards and promotional material easily accessible.

- Put your new contacts into your database, detail your notes on the note pad, and designate your next action item with this person.

- Attend one networking function per week.

- Provide quality leads and referrals to others and others will do the same for you.

- If you're making up a "Hello My Name Is…" name tag, write your name in large bold letters and place it on your right shoulder. During a handshake, the right shoulder naturally moves in with the outstretched hand so the receiver's eyes follow that line. This helps the other person find your name more easily. If you have an official company name tag, all the better. This implies that you're a pro at what you do, not just passing through a career on the way to something else.

What networking group would you like to join?

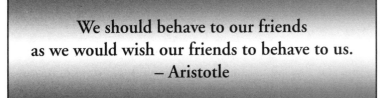

**We should behave to our friends
as we would wish our friends to behave to us.
– Aristotle**

39. Dine for Fun and Profit

Business meals are more than meet the eye. Not only is food on the menu, but your conversation is as well. Meals are great opportunities to multi-task—covering a business agenda, eating, and building relationships. When you share a meal, you open up opportunities for casual conversation that allows the formation of deep and meaningful bonds.

One day a business acquaintance who I genuinely liked and admired invited me for lunch. She told me that she wanted to build the referral side of her business and asked if I would help. "I'd be delighted," I said. I would bring my contact list. She chose the restaurant—a fast food Thai café in her neighborhood. I drove 35 minutes to meet her; she drove five. I don't do spicy food; she assured me it wasn't.

While perched on a tall wooden stool, I choked down fire food and gave her dozens of referrals. I was going through my entire database, so her constant urging for more became annoying. I paid for my own lunch (she did not offer). There was no thank you note sent afterwards, nor any sign of appreciation—not for the time I was giving her, the drive, paying for the meal, and the referrals themselves. Instead of feeling helpful, I felt abused.

It was the little things that left a very bad taste in my mouth. I would have gladly continued to send referrals her way had it not been for the ill-mannered way she handled asking.

Here are some etiquette guidelines for business meals in order to put your best, er, "fork" forward and build strong relationships that result in increased referrals.

Planning:

If you're inviting a guest, your role is to select the date, time, and restaurant, send out the invitation(s), make the reservations, decide where and how you will meet your guests, *pay for the meal*, and plan the seating.

a. Select the date, time, and restaurant.
    Don't try a new restaurant unless it's been given rave reviews. Choose a location that has a variety of selections to accommodate your guest's tastes. Stay away from your company's business hangout— you don't want to feel intimidated by watchful eyes or office politics. Also stay away from restaurants boasting fast service—you don't want to feel rushed. Keep a file of good restaurants handy or call the concierge at an upscale local hotel. They're paid to know what's good.

b. Send out the invitation(s).
    If you're hosting the lunch, send out the invitation a week or two in advance and give choices for time and day. Your invitation should include directions to the location, where you will be, and what you will be wearing (if you haven't met). Make it clear in your invitation that you're buying to avoid an awkward scene over the tab. Lunch invitations are safer than dinner because they don't encroach on personal time and territory. When you invite your guest, be sure that she understands the purpose of the meeting and the agenda. Let your invitee know who else will be there and if specific materials should be brought along. You can go "dutch" and split the bill with people you know very well. If you're the one being invited and you're unsure of who's picking up the tab, you might ask at payment time, "How much is my half?" Or, "How about if we split this?" Or, "Let me

pick this one up. Next time, your treat?" At the very
least, offer to pay the tip and/or valet.

c.   Make the reservations.
     If your meeting is important (as mine seemed to be to
     my friend), choose a restaurant that's important
     enough to require reservations—not fast food.

d.   Decide where you will greet your guest(s).
     Arrive before the scheduled time. If anyone's on a
     fixed schedule, this should be made clear in advance.
     Have your coat checked before guests arrive. If it's a
     large gathering, wait until everyone has arrived before
     being seated. If one or two people are over 10 minutes
     late, it's acceptable to be escorted to a table and order
     drinks. Let the maitre d' lead so that you, the host,
     may follow the group at the rear.

e.   Plan the seating.
     Give the best seat—the one that faces out to the
     restaurant—to your guest. The seat to the right of the
     host is reserved for the guest of honor.

Ordering:
Alcohol is generally not ordered with lunch. If your guest
orders a drink, you should order one too so that your guest
will not drink alone. If your guest declines alcohol, you
should too. If you don't want to drink alcohol, order something else. If you don't know how to select wine, ask the
sommelier or waiter for a recommendation. When ordering
the meal, make suggestions about the specialties of the house
if you know them. It's also polite to mention what sounds
good in order to help your guest feel comfortable ordering
within a price range. You might say, "The lobster with saffron
sounds terrific." If you're a guest, order in the mid price range
68

to show respect for the host.

Ask your guest if s/he is ready to order and say to the waiter, "My guest is ready to order." This signals who gets the bill at the end of the meal. Don't order something you're not sure how to eat or something potentially sloppy, such as long pasta, whole lobster, or French onion soup. If your guest orders a soup, salad, appetizer, or dessert, you should too.

Dining Do's and Don'ts	
Don't...	Do...
Talk with your mouth full	Put your purse/brief case on the floor or lap.
Talk business until after meal is ordered	(Put the leg of your chair through strap
Criticize the food or service	Pass salt and pepper together
Wave your food around on a utensil	Eat slowly with your mouth closed
Reach across the table	Hold a glass with all fingers of one hand on the glass
Say "I'm stuffed."	Cut lemons before squeezing
Rest elbows on the table until after eating	Use a small leather notebook for taking notes
Raise your voice	Place papers on the seat next to you instead of the table.

40. Network with Your Competition

Your competition is a terrific source of referrals. Networking with your competition means that people of identical or similar businesses refer each other when (for whatever reason) they cannot accommodate a customer's needs.

Let's say you're a contractor. Another contractor may be asked to work on a home remodel but cannot take the work because of an overloaded schedule. If you're networking with this contractor, there's a good chance he'll refer you when he cannot take the work. Then when you're in the same situation, you'll refer business to him.

Speakers, doctors, lawyers, realtors and many other professionals enjoy increased business by changing the paradigm and looking at their competitors as their allies. If a client asks for something out of your range of expertise, refer the work to someone who can provide it. We should all be in business together working to serve our customers.

What competitors would you feel comfortable referring?

_____

_____

> To be good is noble;
> but to show others how to be good
> is nobler and no trouble.
> – Mark Twain

41. Expand Your Circle of Influence

Referrals increase when you increase your Circle of Influence. Influence is the degree of power you have in affecting outcomes with other people, things, or a course of events. Influence can be increased through assertiveness, passiveness, aggression, and persuasion. It is also affected by:

1. Position   3. Prestige

2. Wealth   4. Ability

Your network is designed to build referrals but without some level of *positive* influence in that network your time and effort will bear little fruit for anyone.

Many people have a difficult time coming to terms with influence or power. I am one of them. I grew up in a household that advocated humility. Unfortunately, power's gotten a bad rap because of the people who've abused it. Everyone has some degree of personal power. When we allow it to flourish, it means we're using *all* of our assets to manifest change. When that power is misguided, it can do a great deal of harm. When it's used for good, miracles can happen. Some people have influenced our thinking and actions for hundreds, even thousands of years!

You have much more influence than you realize. The movie, *It's a Wonderful Life,* made this abundantly clear. Your power reaches out to others in an imaginary circle. When you increase that circle of influence, you extend not only your network but also your ability to make a difference. Your network has the capacity to be an ever-expanding universe of

71

alliances. It also means that you can help more people, which naturally evolves into more referrals. Successful people work on increasing their circle of influence. You can do this by increasing your effectiveness in four areas:

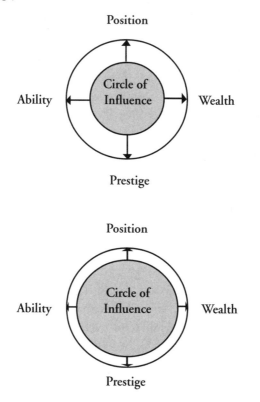

Each one of these "influencers" might seem a bit intimidating to tackle as a "project," but the fact is that you're *already* exerting some degree of influence in each area. Furthermore, many of the ideas presented in this book will enable you to expand the circle as well. This concept helps you organize your thinking and bring awareness to what might seem like a mysterious phenomenon. Since we said that the first strategy for increasing referrals is to be strategic, let's apply that principle and begin to expand your influence now.

1. **Position:**
   This area refers to your social standing, status, title, or rank. What next step do you need to make in order to improve your position? (Run for office, ask for a promotion, rename your current title, get a job?)

2. **Wealth:**
   Wealth is more than money. It's also having an abundance of valuable resources at your disposal or simply feeling good about what you do.

   a. What resources do you have at your disposal that you're under-utilizing?

   b. What personal satisfaction do you feel when helping others?

3. **Prestige:**
   This represents the level of respect, honor, or esteem in which others regard you.

   a. What do you need to do to earn the respect of others (be courageous)?

   b. How can you increase your value to others?

4. **Ability:**
   This is your physical and mental performance. It also includes your natural or acquired skills and talent. Knowledge also increases your ability to perform.

   a. What do you have to change, learn, or develop in order to increase your abilities?

42. Become an Information Navigator

We live in the Information Age but the challenge for many is that there's *too* much information to effectively use it. That's how you can help. Become an information navigator for your customers.

Part of your own personal development should include 30 minutes a day of sifting through newspapers, trade journals, periodicals, magazines, newsletters, or any informative resources to stay current. At the same time, keep an eye out for items that you think your clients might find useful, interesting, or just entertaining. Look for web sites that may be helpful. Then fax or email the items to your clients as a means of staying in touch and providing a value added service.

One successful executive I know made it a habit to connect every piece he reads to one of his clients. This helps him focus on their interests and strengthens the relationship. His thoughtfulness pays off in a steady stream of referrals.

Whether you do it through email or snail mail, send out at least one FYI (For Your Information) a week. Make sure it's relevant to your client's needs and/or taste. Include a note that says something like, "Thought you might be interested in this. Best wishes."

What have you read lately that would help someone else?

 Don't wait for your ship to come in.
Swim out to it!

43. Have a 60 Sec. Commercial Ready

I used to increase the bottom line of businesses by sending them qualified customers. I could have told you that I sold advertising, but advertising isn't what interests people. It's the benefit that people want. We buy solutions that products and services provide *by way of* advertising, real estate, insurance, construction, therapy, brokering etc.

I gave all my prospects their first ads for free—their own 60-second commercial, by asking them to identify:

1. Their name
2. Their organization, type of business or type of work
3. How they help others solve problems

"Hi. My name is Lisa Taylor. My organization, XYZ, makes *relocation a vacation.* We're a turnkey destination manager, finding business sites, organizing, financing, and even packing your belongings. When we move you, moving is hassle free."

If you're saying, "Hi my name is Joe Brown and I sell life insurance," you're missing out on piquing interest in what you REALLY do—helping create wealth and $ independence.

Networking events typically give everyone an opportunity to give a 60-second commercial to the group. Project your voice with confidence. Write the *benefits* of what you do here:

_____

_____

_____

44. Find a Mentor

Everyone needs a mentor—someone who can encourage, advise, and cut down your learning curve. A mentor is *anyone* who gives guidance without advancing his or her own agenda.

Seasoned members of a sales team, those near retirement, or retired pros from your field are ideal choices. They have the experience, the time, and they're not competing with you.

Mentoring can be formal (assigned) or informal (not duty bound). √ Check off those that apply to you now:

Mentor did this for me:	I have done for others:	
_____	_____	Inspire, build confidence, encourage
_____	_____	Share valuable information
_____	_____	Teach by example, coach, counsel
_____	_____	Set high standards and expectations
_____	_____	Listen and make recommendations
_____	_____	Offer challenges and support
_____	_____	Stand by you in times of need

Who can help you?   Who can you mentor?

_____   _____

Working together works!

45. Speak in the Positive

People like being around positive people. It improves morale, increases endorphins (feeling of well-being), and heightens energy. A pro is someone who finds a way to express herself using "Yes" language instead of "No" language.

If someone wants you to return a call by 2 PM and you're unavailable then, say what you *can* do, not what you *can't.* "I'm in a meeting at 2 and I *can* get back to you by 3. Is that good for you?" Don't say, "I *can't* get back to you at 2:00 but I'll call you at three." The difference is subtle, but it sends a message that says you're either cooperative or not. No one cares about what you *can't* do, only what you *can.*

If you ran a retail store and didn't want people bringing in food, you could put up a negative sign that reads, "No Food Allowed," or a positive message that reads, "Please enjoy your food outside the store." Which one makes you feel better about shopping there?

Rather than being negative about the competition, help your prospects to understand why your product or service is a better fit for their needs. A simple comparison of features and benefits will speak for itself. Find something supportive to say. "They offer a good product, and here's how we differ..."

If you spend your valuable time running down a competitor with your prospects, you raise the unsettling question in their mind: If this is what you have to say about so-and-so, what are you saying about me behind *my* back?

Everyday, be your best.
Let the rest of the world, take care of the rest.

46. Be Prompt

If you want to show respect for others, earn *their* respect by allowing ample time to arrive at meetings or appointments. time. If you have trouble being punctual, try setting your watch five or ten minutes ahead and live your life ahead of others. You'll be relieved when you can actually cash in on those extra minutes, especially when stuck in traffic. I've been setting all of my clocks five minutes fast for over fifteen years. Many times I've been able to buy myself time and peace of mind by knowing I have a few minutes to spare.

Another aspect of promptness is developing a sense of urgency in all that you do. Respond to all correspondence in 24 - 48 hours. Return *all* phone calls within 24 hours. Promptly follow up on all requests for information. If your schedule doesn't permit, be sure to delegate retrieval and response of your messages and correspondence to another while you're unavailable. If you're unable to respond fully, at least acknowledge the message or letter and let the other person know when you'll get back to them. It's just common courtesy.

Remember, the person trying to reach you could be a referral. Putting your best foot forward is critical. You only get one chance to make a good first impression.

Promptness tells the public that you're professional, organized, and responsible. Those are the characteristics of someone you can depend upon and would be happy to recommend.

 People don't arrive late. They leave late!

47. Give Referrals to Others

If you recognize an opportunity to provide referrals to a prospect or customer, take the initiative and do it. Your contact will be grateful and may reciprocate by providing you with referrals as well.

As you establish your reputation, you'll also find yourself in the position where others are asking *you* for referrals. This shows that others respect your judgment. Don't jeopardize that respect by making a bad referral.

If you don't have complete confidence in someone's integrity or ability, don't offer the name up just to show that you have contacts. You make yourself worthy of referrals not only by the way you conduct yourself and your work, but also with whom you associate. If you send someone off to do business with an incompetent or unethical person, you do an injustice to three people: the customer who needs the referral, the person who received the referral (not a good fit), and the person who made the referral—you.

Who in your network do you feel comfortable referring?

_____

_____

_____

 If you're too busy to help those around you succeed, you're too busy.

48. Mix Business with Pleasure

I once talked with a successful RV salesman who says that the *one* reason for his success was mixing business with pleasure. He always made sure that his prospects enjoyed their RV experience with him.

When a prospect wanted to take a test drive, he would put them in the driver's seat and guide them to a beautiful lake where they would "drop anchor" and sit in the peace and quiet of the shade trees. There, among the birds and quiet lapping of the water, he would break out the snacks—cheese, crackers, sodas, wine, pickles, chips—good-time food. They would settle back into the moment and enjoy each other's company. By giving his prospects a sample of the experience, this man was able to move prospects into their future—and it was always a pleasurable one with his RVs.

Because of his giving nature, positive attitude, ability to mix business with a pleasurable experience, he was not only the top producer, but also received more referrals than anyone else in the county.

How can you mix business with pleasure for your prospects?

_____

_____

_____

_____

_____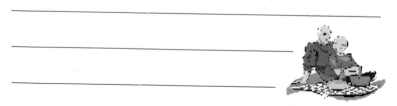

49. Be Easy to Find

You are a treasure, so don't be the kind that's buried. Be easy to find so that others can get in touch with you.

I was once asked to speak to the Lion's Club Leadership Forum where over 3,000 Lion's Club leaders would be in attendance. I wanted to learn more about the organization but unfortunately I had a hard time finding any local contacts for conducting my research. I called the Chamber of Commerce in three cities but found no phone number or chapter listing. I looked in the phone book and called directory information—no number. I called 800 information—no listing. I called the mayor's office—no listing. If it hadn't been for their website, I would have been at a total loss.

When I gave my speech, I asked the members why they were so hard to find, especially when one of their issues was sagging membership. Not everyone has Internet hookups nor would they think to check for a site. I told them of my struggles and they agreed it was a problem, but they were stymied as to what to do. Their work is of tremendous value, especially in helping the blind, but unfortunately it's difficult to join without a referral contact.

Be easy to do business with by being easy to find. Always carry business cards and information request cards with you. Get listed in all of the relevant directories, both general and specific to your industry. Have an email address that's easy to remember and your website listed on as many search engines as you can afford.

The greatest good we can do for others is not to share our riches but to reveal theirs.

50. Tell the Good, Bad and the Ugly

A real estate agent once told me that she had an undying loyalty working with a particular lender for one reason — honesty. Whenever there was a glitch in the loan process, the lender would immediately inform her.

"Both my clients and I need to know the truth of what's going on. There are always snags in buying a home, but I can't help my buyers if my hands are tied with false hopes and delays. I want to minimize the uncertainty."

Studies show that people want to know the facts. If you have to deliver bad news, try the sandwich approach:

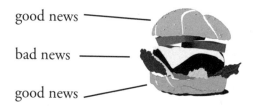

good news

bad news

good news

Everyone knows you're using a standard technique, but they still like the balance of good with the bad. If you have something sensitive or difficult to say, buffer it with:

"This isn't easy for me to say..." or
"I'm sorry to have to tell you..."

Buffering helps people brace themselves for the worst. Usually the news isn't half as bad as what they have imagined.

The truth will set you free, but first it will tick you off.

51. Gilt by Association

The expression, "It's not what you know, but who you know" is an unfortunate reality. We'd like to think that our talents and expertise are enough to create successes, but the fact is that connections can make or break your ability to manifest your talents on a larger scale.

Knowing the right people in positions of influence can add directly to your bottom line. It could be a manager, a business owner, CEO, a politician, or a celebrity. Your affiliation with respected influential people follows the logic that if they value their association with you, your aura of importance increases-- "gilt" by association. Because of this relationship, others will place a higher value on what you do.

How do you meet influential people? Once you become an expert, one strategy is to invite a prominent person to partici-pate in a research or writing project. Decide on an area of mutual interest, then contact your "influencer" and ask for his advice, comments, or an interview. When you make the contact, keep your discussion to the topic at hand. Once the project is under way, keep your contact abreast of progress. If you use your expert's exact words in your project, give the person a chance to review or amend them.

A friend of mine implemented this idea. In the course of one year, she called on company CEOs and Presidents for their stories to include in her book. Her circle of influence has expanded to hundreds of "movers and shakers" while her personal income has grown to over a million dollars a year.

With whom would you like to be affiliated?

52. Work the Referral

Referrals are wonderful but they must be worked. This means you (or the referring source) still have to make a call to the referred person. You need to follow up on that call ASAP, and then work the lead like any other sales event. One of the best ways to organize this work is by using the sales funnel.

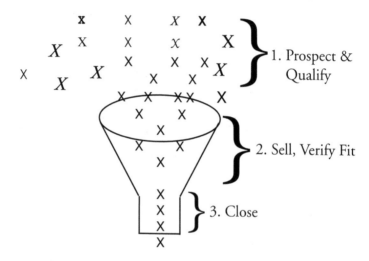

There are three parts to the funnel that represent three types of sales activity. The work above the funnel is prospecting and qualifying. This represents enormous opportunities. Referrals sift through this area, helping you identify qualified prospects quickly so that you can move them inside the funnel sooner.

Inside the funnel are semi-qualified leads. Do your typical sales activity to verify the fit and bring in the sale—appointments, demonstrations, proposals, meeting decision makers.

The bottom contains all contacts that you expect to close in half of the sales cycle. The type of work here is closing—you know the next steps to be taken.

When you *suspect* a qualified prospect, move her from above the funnel to inside. You may have dozens of contacts there that you'll track throughout the process. If some of your prospects fall out of the funnel, it's for one of two reasons:

1. Conditions: These are legitimate reasons for not buying that actually exist—going out of business, moving, or lack of money to buy. Thank the prospect for their time and move on.

2. Objections: These are reasons for not buying *based on a lack of information.* Know the objections for your product or services and resolve them early in the sale so that they're a non-issue.

You may use the funnel to allocate sales time, track sales activity, and prevent the roller coaster effect—the uneven flow of sales. The only way to prevent the roller coaster effect is to work the funnel in the following order:

1. Closing
2. Prospecting & Qualifying
3. Selling, Verifying Fit

Close the business in the first part of your day, then move on to prospecting, then selling. You must keep a steady stream of qualified prospects in the funnel in order to keep steady sales.

You may also use the 80/20 formula to allocate time. If you invest 20% of your time on your top priority, you should be 80% effective. Twenty percent of an eight hour day is a little over an hour and half. If you want to be 100% effective, double your time in that area. According to the formula, invest 1.6 hours closing, at least 1.6 hours prospecting and then you'll have the remainder of the day left for "selling."

53. Prospect When You Don't Need To

I once knew a top producing financial consultant whose sales funnel was always brimming with qualified contacts. He knew that he could stay busy just selling within his funnel (see #52), but he also realized that the secret to his success was prospecting when he didn't need to.

Every day he would make ten calls to new prospects—without fail. Most of them were referrals, so his call back ratio was very high. To be sure he made his calls before the day got hectic, they became a ritual first thing in the morning.

Over the years his book of business grew to the point where his assistants did everything except his big-ticket sales. His business was self-renewing, not only because he delegated and enlisted the help of others, but also because he kept in constant contact with what he called, "new blood."

There's a natural attrition with customers—some move away, retire, resign, or lose their need for what you offer. To keep your business alive, infuse yours with new blood everyday.

What are your next steps for contacting 10 new leads a day?

_____

_____

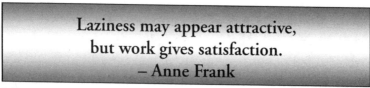

Laziness may appear attractive,
but work gives satisfaction.
– Anne Frank

54. Send a Report

Whenever you've completed a high-profile project or brought in a big-ticket sale, you may want to issue a final report or press release to appropriate members on your contact list. If you send out a newsletter, include it as a news item or issue an email update to your other customers.

Show the world that you're not only working, but working on things of importance. Lots of people subscribe to the notion that if you want to get something done, give it to a busy person. Let your contacts know how busy you are, but also that your business has expanded in order to accommodate even more customers.

If your customer or client will also be sending out a report, that's added visability. Your name will be broadcast into a new circle of influence. Also ask your clients if you may have copies of their reports to distribute yourself.

The act of sending out reports will not only enhance your professional image, but also serve as a silent referral that flies in under the radar.

What have you done lately that warrants a report or press release? What's your next step?

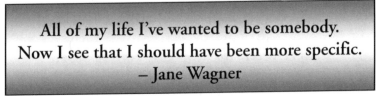

All of my life I've wanted to be somebody.
Now I see that I should have been more specific.
– Jane Wagner

55. Prospect Your Past

We all have people in our past who are gold mines of opportunity. Renewing relationships may seem awkward, but many people enjoy hearing from old acquaintances. People naturally wonder, "Whatever happen to...." You not only answer that question, but also open up potential business.

Make a list of your past acquaintances in groups such as:

- schools
- colleges
- jobs
- neighborhoods

- clubs
- churches
- teams
- associations

Start by getting current contact information. There are many internet resources that can help you find missing people. When you call, make this a conversational session so that there's a back and forth exchange. The purpose of this contact is to learn about the *other* person. If you're doing all the talking, you'll never learn anything (see #6).

When I moved from Thousand Oaks to San Diego, I decided to update my database. I called on every entry, explaining that I was updating my contact files. For any contacts I didn't know well, I simply asked if they still used my type of services "once in awhile." I was astounded at how many contacts wanted to do more business. You can help your contacts solve *current* problems by prospecting your past. They'll be glad to hear from you. They've probably wondered where you went.

Top producers do what 80% of the people are not willing to do.

56. Send Referral Rewards Newsletters

Create and distribute a free monthly, bimonthly, or quarterly referral reward newsletter. Newsletters generally consist of short paragraphs, containing helpful information, news updates, editorial commentary, pithy quotations, items you've personally found useful, quick tips from others, or how-to's on subjects of mutual interest. What makes a referral rewards newsletter different is that it highlights referrals you've been given, referrals you've given to others (with their permission), and provides information on a "Referral Reward Program."

The realtor who sold us our home five years ago sends me his newsletter every other month. It's so informative that I read all eight pages. His newsletter is called, "Frank's Home News: News to Help You Save Time and Money." The newsletter arrived for Father's Day so the front-page not only had a table of contents, but also a piece on the history of Father's Day, and a poem about dads.

Here's what else Frank included: How to Teach Responsibility, Valuable Tips for Protecting Lap Tops from Theft, Humorous Police Quotes, How to Use Technology to Lose Weight, Taking Control of Clutter, 10 Tips on How to Win Friends and Influence People, Words of Wisdom, contests to win, thank you notices for referrals he's received, a featured business of the month, a client of the month, one page called Free Information Fax Form, Trivia Quiz of the Month with dinner prizes, and the last page had details on his Referral Reward Program. Here's the program text he printed on the back page, "above the fold:"

Referral Reward Program

I want to thank those of you who have participated in my Client Referral Program! Like any company, I need new clients to stay in business. Over the years, I've found that looking for new clients takes away from the time I would rather spend working for you and other clients.

If I helped you in the sale or purchase of real estate then you know how well I serve my clients. If you refer your friends and relatives to me, everybody benefits. I can serve you better. I send you a nice gift. And I assure you that I'll take the very best care of any friends or family that you refer my way. For more information about my Referral Reward Program, give me a call at ..... It's a great program where, as my way of saying, "Thanks," I send you a token of my appreciation for recommending me.

If you would like any of your friends, coworkers, relatives and business acquaintances to receive a FREE subscription to this newsletter, please fill out the information on the previous page. I'll also send them a note with their first issue telling them that you suggest they receive the newsletter and to contact me if they would like to stop at any time. If you enjoy this newsletter, share it with people you know, with no hassle for you!

(Reprinted with permission of Frank Grangetto)

The indirect message you communicate through a high quality newsletter will do the advertising for you and increase your chances of having your name passed on to others.

57. Give Nickels and Dimes

Ben Franklin coined the expression "penny-wise and pound foolish." Its wisdom is unarguable.

I used to do business with a company that rented out professional development cassette tapes. I enjoyed the programs so much that I referred many of my clients to him over the years. I didn't get commissions from the referrals—I did it simply because I believed in the value of drive-time learning.

Since we frequently talked on the phone, it seemed odd that the owner never mentioned the referrals. He would also bill me for many petty, add-on charges—a $2 extra shipping fee here, a $1 charge there—nickel and diming ad infinitum.

Unless you're running a hospital where every aspirin is billable, don't quote fees or invoice your services in a way that communicates pettiness. Most feel these small charges should already be included in the fee they're paying.

Because of the lack of responsiveness, I began to feel that my referrals weren't appreciated. I wasn't looking for special treatment, but I also never got any positive feedback. Just once it would have been nice to hear, "You've been such a good customer and referred so many people to us that we're going to waive the extra postage required on this package as our way of saying thank you." After awhile I found another tape rental source. One year later he was out of business.

> Doing nothing for others
> is the undoing of ourselves.
> – Horace Mann

58. Be Generously Selective

When referrals start to steadily come your way, it means that you've reached a high level of competence—not only in your work but also how you work the referrals. Demonstrating competence is a valued quality that people look for before making a referral. When others believe that you're good at what you do and that your products or services are in demand, the irony is that they send more business your way.

Catch 22

You start getting more referrals than you can handle when you no longer need them.

When your business starts to skyrocket, you won't have time to work all the incoming referrals. Now it's time to become selective in how you spend your time and energy. You'll need to make two important decisions at this point: which referrals to keep and which ones to refer to others.

If you can't work all of your referrals, be generous with your selection. Instead of casting off those you can't accommodate, refer them to someone else who can. Every referral is a potential gold mine for someone else.

Who can you refer to someone else right now?

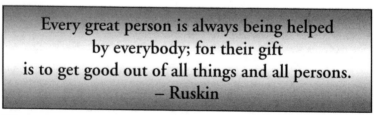

Every great person is always being helped
by everybody; for their gift
is to get good out of all things and all persons.
– Ruskin

59. Stay Within Yourself

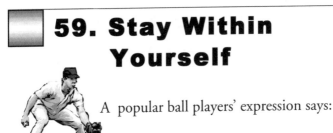

A popular ball players' expression says:

Stay within yourself.

In baseball this means find out what you're good and stay with it. In business it means only providing goods and services that are in your area of expertise.

If you develop a reputation for constantly delivering quality products and services, others may think that you're capable of walking on water, or at least handling *any* problem or situation that crops up. They may ask you to perform other services for which you're not qualified or refer you to others claiming that you can work "miracles."

Don't fall into the trap of saying "Yes" to everyone. Avoid work that's out of your area of expertise, no matter how tempting it may be for you to maintain the illusion that you can do any and everything.

True, miracles do happen, and it's good to stretch your learning, but don't go to school on your customers until you're ready. If you have to make a big stretch out of your comfort zone, refer the work to someone who's proficient in this area. You may even be able to set up a mentoring program under the tutelage of your referral. If you take on work that's beyond your talents, delivering successful results will be beyond you as well.

Endings are the start of a new journey.

93

60. Provide Feedback on Your Referrals

It's common courtesy to thank others for the referrals they give you. It's also important to give feedback to your referring parties. Effective feedback forms a cycle. Let your source know how things are going or how the transaction went. They have a vested interest in what you're doing and want to know that it was a mutually beneficial connection.

Providing feedback is not only common courtesy, but it stimulates additional referrals in the future. People tend to repeat behaviors that get positive feedback.

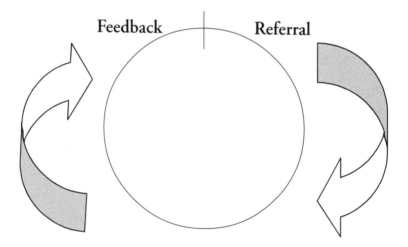

Bring the cycle full circle.

In the middle of every difficulty lies opportunity.
– Albert Einstein

61. Be a Seamless Conversationalist

A seamless communicator is one who is comfortable communicating with anyone. You know how to enter a conversation tactfully, engage in all levels of talk from "small" to "big," help others feel comfortable, and politely exit a conversation.

When you're working a room, it helps everyone to feel more relaxed and referral minded if you know how to smoothly converse. The goal here is to help *others* feel comfortable and valued, *showing a genuine interest in what they have to say.* Unless you've learned the art of talk, especially challenging "small talk," it can be the most stressful part of your day.

If you want to make more effective connections, it's important to be more clear than clever. When you approach someone, be sure to introduce yourself first if he or she doesn't know who you are. Also help others to remember you with a memory jog such as, "Hi. Bill Smith. We met last year at the national convention." If you use questions as part of your introduction, you can help engage others immediately.

Conversation Starters When You Don't Know Anyone:
Perhaps you're at a Chamber of Commerce mixer for the first time and you're feeling a bit uneasy, but you're also there to meet people. Set your fear aside for now and find someone else who is alone. Be a host by initiating a conversation with a smile and words such as:

- "Hi. My name is Bill Smith. (Shake hands.) And you are...? This is my first time here. Are you new or a regular?" (Be sure to listen to the name. If you didn't get it say, "I'm sorry. I didn't quite catch your name..."

- "Hi. My name is Bill Smith. This is a terrific event. Did you run into that traffic jam on the 405?"
- Have you been a member long?
- What do you do when you're not at…(a seminar, conference, mixer, party etc.)
- How long have you been in your career?
- Where are you from? What's it like there?

"Small talk" is "safe talk." But small things can lead to bigger and better things, including stimulating conversations, valuable new friends, and new referrals. Hang in there.

How to Enter a Group Conversation:

1. Go up to the group and stand slightly outside of the gathering, but not so far outside that your presence isn't noticed. It's like politely knocking on a door.

2. Listen to learn the topic of conversation until you feel comfortable that you can make a contribution.

3. When the conversation hits a lull, you may then politely make a contribution. When talk slows down and group members are thinking about a new point of interest, one or two will turn your way and include you in the inner circle. You may also flat out ask, "May I join you?"

4. Introduce yourself to the group and if the topic is still going, ask a question about the topic or make a contribution.

Continued on the next page | ▮▮▮➡

5.   Ask questions to learn about the others' interests, needs, wants, and preferences. They are teaching you valuable information that will help you to help them. If you're overly talkative, or begin a side talk with a group member, you'll alienate, not befriend.

6.   Offer your business card if a connection is made and ask for cards from others. Don't rush into talking about your business unless asked to do so. It's more polite to show an interest in others first.

What to Say in Conversations:

Any group conversation should be all-inclusive, meaning that everyone in the group should be able to participate in the topic. When conversations become so targeted that a participant can't join in, it's rude to continue. On the other hand, if the topic is new to you, small talk in conversations can be a valuable way to learn. Instead of withdrawing, you might say, "I'm sorry. I missed that in the news. What happened?" Or "I don't play golf, but I've always wanted to know more...

Here is a list of PC topics of conversations:

Safe Topics	_Unsafe Topics_
Weather	Personal Problems
Traffic	Yours or Other People's Health
Travel	Off-Color/Questionable Jokes
Books	Gossip
Environment	Personal Income
Common Interest/Experience	Intimate Personal Details
Compliments	Criticisms
Non-Controversial News	Cost of Goods/Services
Sports, the Oscars, Arts,	Office Politics
Music, Science	
Misc: Hobbies, Exercise, Cars	
Your Business!	

You can always keep a conversation going by asking open-ended questions. These help you to control the course of the conversation and "host" the topic. "Speaking of growth, what ever happened to the town renovation project?" Open-ended questions cannot be answered with a "Yes," or "No," but invite more detailed information. They always begin with:

1. Who   4. Where
2. What   5. Why
3. When   6. How

After introductions you might ask, "How long have you been an architect? What inspired you to get into the business? Where are you located? What are some of the projects you've worked on lately? What are some of the challenges you run into? What kind of clients do you look for?" When you ask questions, each should logically flow from the answer. People love to give advice and talk about what they're good at.

Here are some additional suggestions for conversations:

"I wonder if you'd be willing to share some of your expertise (experiences) with me. I have a situation... (explain). How would you handle it?"

"You seem to know quite a few people. Who can you recommend for..."

"I could really use your advice on the best way to move forward on a new project. (Explain.) What do you recommend?

"I really value your input."

"How do you feel about...?"

How to Exit a Group Conversation:
One goal of group gatherings is to increase your connections so it doesn't pay to stay in one place and monopolize someone's time. Respect the rules of networking and mingle, but know how to leave a conversation graciously.

1. Wait for a laugh in the conversation. "Leave 'em laughing" is an old expression that creates a natural, positive, upbeat break between people. "It's been a pleasure. (Handshake.) Looking forward to learning more about what you do."

2. Wait for a lull in the conversation before excusing yourself with something like, "Excuse me. I don't want to occupy all of your time. It's been a pleasure meeting you. I look forward to seeing you again in the future." Shake hands, smile, and depart. Heading for the refreshment table is always a safe destination when you don't know where to go next.

3. If there are just two involved, you might say, "Now that I know more about what you do, I think you'd enjoy talking with Phil. Have you met Phil Miller? Let me introduce you." If you don't know anyone else in the room, suggest that you both join another group or someone else who is alone.

4. If you're new, head over to the refreshment table and introduce yourself to the first person you see, perhaps with a comment about the "great spread."

The name of the game is how many people can you meet and get to know. If you make more connections, you'll make more friends, create more leads, and earn more referrals.

Here is a conversational goal checklist. The next time you find yourself with an opportunity to communicate, either individually or at a networking event, be seamless:

◊ Meet three people a day who can directly help you achieve your referral goals.

◊ Meet three people who can indirectly help you achieve your referral goals.

◊ Meet someone who is a member of an association (a different one if you are at one).

◊ Meet someone who has been in his or her industry for more than ten years.

◊ Meet someone who shares common interests with you (movies, sports, hobbies)

◊ Meet someone who lives within ten miles of you.

◊ Meet someone who is in your industry.

◊ Meet someone who is a member of a service or community group.

> **A single conversation across the table with a wise man is worth a month's study of books.**
> **– Chinese Proverb**

62. Set Stretch Goals

A goal is a dream with a deadline. Stretch goals take a conservative wish and push it to the limit. When you ask more of yourself, you'll be astounded at what you can deliver. If your goal is to earn *one* referral at the end of a sale, stretch it to *five*. You may not reach five, but you'll earn more than one.

A way to remember the components of a well-formed goal is to make them S.M.A.R.T.

S: Be specific. Name exactly *what* you plan to accomplish. Example: increase referrals

M: Make it measurable. How can you track progress? Example: increase referrals by 10% or earn five new

A: Make it action oriented. Give your statement a verb. Example: Here I've chosen *increase* and *earn* for verbs.

R: Make it realistic: Set stretch but doable goals. Example: It's realistic to meet five people a day, or ask for five referrals at the end of a sale.

T: Time Defined. Specify a date, time period or deadline. Example: Increase referrals 10% by the end of each month. Or earn five referrals after each sale by using the ideas in this book.

Test your goal setting power by answering the questions in this assessment. Give yourself 5 points for each Yes (Y), 3 for each sometimes (S), and 0 for each No (N).

Y	S	N	
			1. Do you have SMART stretch goals written for your current referral activities?
			2. Do you follow up with new contacts in a timely manner (within a week)?
			3. Do you schedule a regular time each week to reconnect with people you've haven't communicated with in awhile?
			4. Do you have a consistent written schedule of referral building activities?
			5. Do you schedule recreational down time for yourself each week?
			6. At networking events, do you leave with the names of at least three new contacts who might be potential resources for referrals?
			7. Do you have an organized, effective way of storing and accessing information about your contacts, including their careers, hobbies, and special interests?
			8. Do you use local resources such as newspapers and bulletins to keep on top of new networking or referral opportunities?
			9. Do you regularly seek ways of helping other business contacts to build their referrals?
			10. Do you have at least one meal a week scheduled for referral building activity?

Score:

40 – 50 = Excellent! Keep up the great work.

25 – 39 = Good. Keep adding to your goals.

0 – 24 = A nice start. Set more referrals goals.

Once you've set the stretch goal, schedule it into your calendar in the form of an activity. If the goal is complex, you may need to break it down into smaller steps called objectives.

Goals may be short term (within a day or week), mid term (within a month or two) or long range. Take a moment to write a few S.M.A.R.T. goals here to get you started.

Three Long-Term Goals:

1. _____

2. _____

3. _____

Break one of your long-term goals into the smaller supporting goals you will need to accomplish to reach the long term goal.

Three Short-Term Supporting Goals:

1. _____

   _____

2. _____

   _____

3. _____

   _____

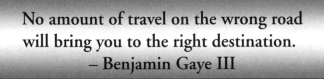

No amount of travel on the wrong road will bring you to the right destination.
– Benjamin Gaye III

63. Follow Through

When I travel, I exercise on the computerized rowing machines in hotels. These machines display a pacer boat and your boat on a monitor, the goal being to row in sync with the pacer boat. Since I'm not crazy about exercising in the first place, I've always tried to row faster than the pacer boat to get it over with. For every pacer stroke, I made two.

For the longest time I couldn't understand why I was constantly falling behind. No sooner had I started rowing than the computer would read, *You are one boat behind.* Then a few minutes later, *You are five boats behind.* "There must be something wrong with the machine," I thought. "I'm rowing twice as fast and I'm going backwards!" But when every rowboat in every hotel was telling me the same thing, I had to reconsider—maybe the problem was with me.

One day I decided to keep my strokes timed with the pacer. Suddenly the machine was working! I realized that when I rowed fast and furiously, the machine *did not give me credit* for incomplete strokes. When I started at the beginning of a full stroke however, and actually *followed through* with it, the computer counted my efforts.

This was a powerful metaphor for me. We can move around a lot, but none it amounts to anything until we follow through—a phone call, an email, an agreement, a service appointment, a good will visit or any other "wrap-up" activity to previous work. Don't let fast activity wear you out. Keep moving, but move completely from start to finish.

 If you don't follow through on what you do, none of the moving counts.

64. Have a Creative Lookout Tower

Always be on the lookout for creative ways to generate leads and referrals. Start an imaginary "lookout tower" that scans the horizon for…

1. **New start-ups**
   New companies often choose to work with the first vendor/supplier that walks through the door. Find new organizations in your area, make an introductory contact, and become an immediate resource for them.

2. **Legal notices**
   Look for new homes, births, new business filings, and other legal notices. These changes often signal a need for your product or services.

3. **Want ads**
   Find out which organizations in your area are hiring. This implies growth and expansion. When companies grow, they need additional products and services.

4. **Charity auctions**
   Attend charity auctions and give a sample of your product or service as your donation. This is a trifector—making a donation to a worthwhile cause, the winner gets to sample your product or service (the strongest lead you can get), and you may also ask the recipient of your donation to refer you to others.

5. **Local newspaper's business section**
   The business section is full of companies and contact names that could turn into new contacts.

6. **Business directories**

   Cole's, Gayle's, SRDS, the Salesmans' Guide, Hoover's and other business directories list companies, phone numbers, and key contacts. This gives you a person's name to call rather than going in "cold."

7. **Be a billboard**

   Get your company name out there. Get a vanity license plate, put a company bumper sticker on your car, put it on coffee mugs, t-shirts, post-it notes, scratch pads, and key rings. Put your name on golf balls and give them away with a catchy slogan. Put your name out there as much as possible. It's free advertising and interested people will ask for more information on what you do.

In what creative ways can you generate leads and referrals?

_____

_____

_____

_____

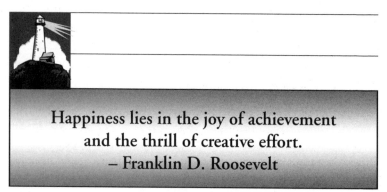

Happiness lies in the joy of achievement and the thrill of creative effort.
– Franklin D. Roosevelt

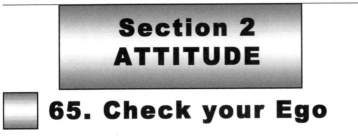

Section 2
ATTITUDE

65. Check your Ego

It's important to have good self esteem. It's quite another to boast your worth to others. The general reaction to those who make it clear to everyone that they, in the immortal words of Reggie Jackson, "are the straw that stirs the drink," is that if you're so good, you don't need any help from me. That translates into "No referrals."

If you work with a client on a project, give credit to all who make a contribution. Post their names in your newsletter, take your team out for lunch and tell them how much you appreciate their efforts. If you think that helping is "part of their job," try a kind word or two. Stand back and watch what happens. When you allow others to participate in the credit, ironically you'll feel better about yourself. Your client will know that you're a team player and be more apt to refer you to others. Also your client (or support staffer who's been promoted since you generously shared the limelight) will also be more likely to ask you back.

Who can you give credit to right now?

> Be daring, be fearless, and don't be afraid
> that somebody is going to criticize or laugh at you.
> If your ego isn't involved, no one can hurt you.
> – R.H.H.

66. Be Professional

Defining professionalism is a bit like the government defining pornography: it's hard to pinpoint but you know it when you see it.

There are many factors that go into being a professional. You can begin to assess your professionalism by taking a good, honest look at yourself and answering questions such as: Do you need to lose weight? Buy some new clothes? Get a haircut? Talk less and listen more? Control your temper?

Here are a number of criteria for helping you assess your professional image. Check off those you'd like to improve:

_	dress/clothing	_	resourcefulness
_	grooming	_	respectfulness
_	articulation	_	organized/efficient
_	consideration of others	_	attentiveness
_	ethics	_	continuous learning
_	responsibleness	_	punctuality
_	courteousness	_	listening
_	discipline	_	thoroughness

When I taught school, believe it or not there were days I didn't want to be there. But kids expect you to be present for them 100% everyday, no excuses. This was the best training ground for my career in sales. I learned that professionals have the discipline to show up and be their best, in spite of how they feel inside. Live from within, when you're doing without.

> **A professional is a person who can do his best at a time when he doesn't particularly feel like it.**
> **– Alistair Cooke**

67. Be a Go-Giver

The first coaching suggestion that I put in this book is my personal favorite (see#1, p.4).

> *You will get everything you want*
> *when you increase your contribution to others.*

I have a friend whose business did a 180 when she really grasped the idea that her business wasn't about her, or making money, or climbing to the top. As soon as she shifted her focus from "What can I get?" to "What can I give?" her business took off. She became a go-giver.

Here's how the concept of go-giving works. If you sell real estate, the more people you provide homes for, the more successful an agent you will be. If you sell automobiles, the more people you can provide transportation for, the more successful you will be. The more gardens you groom, the more successful you will be.

What you put out to others comes back either to help you or haunt you. If you give more than you take, your contributions will come back to you tenfold.

Go get 'em by being a go-*giver.*

> When I chased after money, I never had enough.
> When I got my life on purpose and focused on
> giving of myself and everything that arrived into
> my life, then I was prosperous.
> – Wayne Dyer

68. Admit Your Mistakes

Everyone makes mistakes. When you do, you'll be judged more by how you fix them than the mistakes themselves. Customers are more aggravated by apathetic attitudes in resolving mistakes than the actual problem.

My printer once pulled my job off the press because the pressman noticed that the photo was "grainy." The artist was unavailable so the mistake couldn't be fixed immediately, meaning we would miss an important ship date. I'd rather have them catch the mistake though, let me know what's happened, and give me the option of fixing it rather than printing 14,000 low-quality brochures--hoping I wouldn't notice. I am so impressed by their damage control that I will refer anyone looking for printing services their way.

People of good character admit when they're wrong, apologize, and restore the situation. If you make an error that's going to affect a transaction, don't ignore it, hope that someone else will "catch" it, or blame someone else. Fix it ASAP without pointing fingers. If necessary, alert your customer that a snag took place, say how you've resolved the situation, and apologize.

> A man must be big enough to admit his mistakes, smart enough to profit from them, and strong enough to correct them.
> – John C. Maxwell

69. Don't Appear Desperate

Every business in the world has an occasional down cycle. A look at the stock market between 2000-2001 makes that evident. Unexpected market trends, unforeseen market turns and global influencers can and will disrupt even the strongest businesses. If your sales aren't going well at the moment— look at it this way: it's just for the moment.

You may be in a temporary downturn. But telegraphing your desperation only makes matters worse. Whether you're working at the upper corporate level or as a self-employed sales person, ultimately you want people to invest their confidence in you. Appearing desperate for work does nothing for earning confidence nor rebuilding your business.

Unless you're in need of the police or the fire department, looking desperate in business doesn't bear fruit. If you're going to ask for referrals during a downtime, it's important to maintain a relaxed demeanor and tone of voice. Avoid appearing anxious or stressed. Never disclose that your financial and/ or professional security is dependent upon any one referral.

Act as if you're already successful and your focus will actually pull you in that direction. Everyone loves a winner, so be one. You can always fly first class, even if you sit in the 34th row next to the lavatory. It's a state of mind. Stay confident in yourself and others will see it too. Here are three suggestions for rising above an economic downturn in your business:

1. Concentrate on what you do well and do more of it even better.

2. Notice if you need to make changes in your business as a response to unforeseen changes, make those changes, or go do something else. Don't sit idle.

3. Keep a constant focus on helping to solve other people's problems and you will flourish.

4. Never lose hope for the future. Work towards your future making improvements everyday.

The poet John Keats once wrote that people must develop the ability to deal with uncertainties, mysteries, and doubts. In other words, we must be able to withstand ambiguities and things that aren't quite clear. No one knows what the future holds. If you look to your future optimistically though, you empower yourself to act with energy and determination.

Adapt a long-range attitude toward building your career, realizing that there will always be downtimes and set-backs no matter what you do. It's part of life. Don't take a back seat when adversity hits. Always focus on those things that are in your control and do what you *can* do. Keep strong and manage your emotions by keeping active. As Winston Churchill said, "When you're going through hell, *keep going!*"

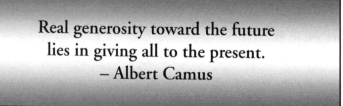

**Real generosity toward the future
lies in giving all to the present.
– Albert Camus**

70. Be Ethical

Aristotle defined good as anything that hit the target for which it was intended. A good putt goes into the hole. A good pass scores a touchdown. So what's a good person? What target are we intended to hit? These are the questions of life. Some believe that the end justifies the means, that if it's a good target (goal), we can do what's needed to pull it off. But while we may accomplish good, we may not be a "good" person if we've performed egregious violations to get it.

Ethics is not just about watching what we do and staying out of trouble. It's about creating strength--inner, interpersonal, and community. Morality is about creating happiness--the best kind that serves and honors us all. What we cultivate in ethics and morality we become--powerful and happy, or weak and unhappy.

This is an enormous subject, full of debate and intrigue. If it were simple, we wouldn't need the court systems. Some believe that ethics and morality came from God. Others believe that groups of people got together to decide on rules of conduct in order to avoid conflict. There is no agreement.

Whatever your belief, inherent within all of us is a basic notion of goodness and fair play. If the purpose of ethics is to live the good life, Dr. Tom Morris suggests we organize the dimensions of the human experience into four:

Dimension	➡	Target
1. Intellectual		Truth
2. Aesthetic		Beauty
3. Moral		Goodness
4. Spiritual		Unity

113

These help us to understand the four targets for promoting happiness in us all. They are also the four foundations for sustaining excellence in what we do.

The ethical and moral dimension has to do with basic goodness, doing what's right, being noble. It enters the realm of justice, selflessness, and kindness. Living by these codes comes from an inner peace and outer harmony. There are moral obligations to ourselves—to develop appropriately and take care of ourselves, and there are moral obligations to others.

If you want to live a happy, good life, it's impossible to create it while performing acts of evil and wrongdoing. It's as simple as that. Living and working by sound principles, morals, and ethics is also critical to building the foundation of an effective referral business. Ethics generally refers to professional obligations and rules of conduct, while morality refers to private behavior. But professional and personal lives are continuous. To be a whole, congruent person, we must integrate the two sides in our behavior. Learn the code of ethics that applies to your profession. If there aren't any, create guidelines for yourself in compliance with what you know to be right, making your conscience your guide.

Some ethical behaviors are covered by company policies, rules, regulations, or the law. Other ethical behaviors are called personal virtues. Here is a partial list:

Fair	Reliable	Insightful
Faithful	Civil	Sensitive
Personal Warmth	Sincere	Empathic
Kindness	Resilient	Hospitable
Creative	Integrity	Truthful
Hopeful	Helpful	Modest
Reasonable	Prudent	Loyal

Committed	Balanced	Principled
Sharing	Enthusiastic	Tolerant
Level-Headed	Humble	Amiable
Cooperative	Benevolent	Tactful
Decent	Consistent	Honest
Dignified	Polite	Graceful

Anyone who questions the efficacy or benefits of these virtues should try living by their opposites. Any normal, right-thinking person could easily see how the effects of harassment, gossiping, politicking, or deceit, for example, could lead to disastrous outcomes. Individuals, organizations, or societies that have flourished and endured over time have done so by continually working to uphold these virtues. We all struggle to consistently live by these qualities, but keeping them top of mind will help to install them as permanent habits in bringing about worthwhile results.

Here are four ways to test your ethics:

1. The Newspaper Test: Avoid doing things that you wouldn't like to see prominently displayed in your local newspaper, especially the headlines.

2. The Role Model Test: What would the person you most respect and admire do in this situation? How would you feel if your most revered mentor could observe your action (parents, coach, reverend, teacher, manager priest, rabbi)?

3. The Mirror Test: Can you look at yourself in the mirror and like what you see?

4. The Morning After Test: Can you live with yourself tomorrow, feeling good about what you did today?

71. Put Your Fears Aside

If you take a close look at why more people don't have more referrals, it usually boils down to fear—fear of asking, fear of failing, fear of change, and even fear of success.

It is said that we're born with two fears. One is the fear of falling and the other is the fear of loud noises. These two fears reduce to one—the fear of the unknown. What we don't know, we fear. Even success can be fearful because it means exchanging the known for the unknown. People who fear changing their status quo live in perpetual unrest of losing it. Fear of failing is a refusal to try new things.

> *The saddest words of tongue or pen are the words,*
> *'it might have been'.*
> — Oliver Wendell Holmes

Fear magnifies uncertainty. Taking a step in any direction can be unsettling, but we pay a heavy price for our fears. It not only costs millions to the bottom line each year, but it's also a powerful obstacle to growth. Fear prevents exploration and learning. It keeps people stuck and inhibits insights or suggestions from circulating. People wind up nervously cautious, afraid to make *any* moves for improvement. This can be fatal in a world that makes adaptation and flexibility a condition of survival. In the end, the greatest mistake we can make is to be in constant fear that one will be made.

When we fear, be it of success, failure, or our own survival, it's difficult to lead our lives to the outcomes we want. Fear manifests itself every day as:

116

- the successful businesswoman who achieves notoriety but cannot lead a balanced life
- the employee doing minimum work for fear of taking a risk or making a mistake
- the housewife who seeks her husband's approval for every purchase
- the man who is intimidated by his wife's independence and personal leadership
- the manager who rules by intimidation
- the sales professional who is afraid to prospect, face rejection, ask for the business, or ask for referrals

Here are some ways to shift focus from the debilitating effects of fear to empowered behaviors that achieve referral results.

1. **Ask questions.**

   Create questions that identify what you want, *without compromise.* By shifting focus from fear to possibility, we can get excited about our future. A mind preoccupied with what *can* be done has no room left for fear.

   Examples:
   - What would you do if you knew you couldn't fail?
   - What project do you want to complete?
   - What problem needs to be solved?
   - What relationship would you like to improve?
   - What misunderstandings exist?
   - What changes would you like to implement?
   - What is too complicated?
   - What takes too long or wears you out?
   - What would you like others to do?
   - What angers you most?
   - What are your unfulfilled goals?
   - What would you like to have happen in your life?

2. **Edit out your internal editor.**

   Don't listen to the internal voice that says, "It's impossible," or "I could never do that." Answer questions boldly and with confidence as if anything were possible. Your belief system is a powerful force that will help pull you in the direction of your goals. If you think you can't do it, you're defeated before you start.

3. **Identify your gaps.**

   Locate the discrepancies between where you are and where you want to be. What is preventing you from closing that distance? Make a list and troubleshoot how you can resolve or diminish the roadblocks. What forces are supporting you? How can you build on those reinforcements?

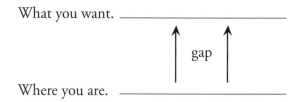

4. **Do what you fear most.**

   Do what you fear and your fear disappears. Since everyone has the capacity to feel fear, the successful are those who face their fear and move forward *anyway.* Confidence comes from doing the things you fear most in order to achieve a record of successful experiences. Confidence leads to courage and courage is the ability to resist temptations to give into fear. It is the mastery of fear, not the absence of it. By rejecting fear, you remove its power to block you. Courage is acknowledging that there is something more important than fear. Action, not thinking, is what overcomes fear.

"You gain strength, experience, and confidence by every experience where you really stop to look fear in the face...you must do the thing you cannot do."
– Eleanor Roosevelt

6. **Love what you do.**
   Has fear ever held you back from what you really wanted? When you believe strongly enough in what you do, fear dissolves. Love drives out fear. The two emotions cannot co-exist in the same space within you. When we lose sight of the ultimate meaning and importance of what we do, we give birth to fear. But enthusiasm sparks greatness. Enthusiasm comes from the root *en theos*—the God within. When you are enthusiastic and love what you do, you manifest your ultimate creative powers.

7. **Focus on successful outcomes.**
   If your goal is to build referrals, focus on what you need to do today and not the emotional concerns. Winners take control by taking chances. Like everyone else, they fear failing, but they refuse to let fear control them. When it comes to making contacts, fear makes strangers of people who should be friends.

What is your greatest fear when it comes to referrals?

What ideas in this book will help you resolve it?

A life lived in fear is a life half lived.

72. Dump Assumptions

During one of my public sales seminars on building referrals, a man in commercial real estate sat next to a woman who sold cosmetics though multilevel marketing. One of the assignments for the day was to meet twenty new people and leave with at least five new referrals and one appointment.

The lender called me the next day to complain. Although there were 250 people in attendance, he said he didn't meet one "decent prospect." I asked, "Who did you meet?" When he gave me the name of the women in multilevel marketing, he threw in a derogatory remark about her career choice, implying that her contacts couldn't *possibly* be of interest in his line of work. He told me that he essentially "blew her off," believing she was a "waste of his time."

"How fortunate that you were able to meet her," I said. "You were the luckiest person in the room. How unfortunate that you didn't take the time to have a conversation with her. You would have learned that she is THE top producer in her organization—one of the most successful MLM's in the world, and that she is married to one of the most influential bankers in Beverly Hills."

"Oh."

Remember the Law of 250 (see #4)? Most people know about 250 people in their circle of influence (see #41). The person sitting next to you may not be able to do business with you, but they may know 250 other people who can. If you think that prospects will fall at your feet in neat bundles, you've got a long wait. If you focus on the apparent issues or limitations of a situation, you'll find limited prospects.

One way to think of opportunity is like looking at an iceberg. Only 1/5 of an iceberg sits above the water line. What's below is massive. Your networking prospects are similar in that what you see (above the water) may not look like an opportunity, but the potential of that contact (below the surface) exists whether we see it or not. It's up to us to put assumptions aside and look below the surface to the hidden potential of each and every situation.

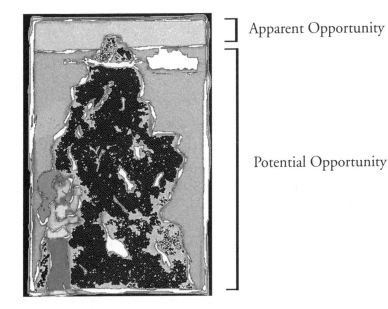

Apparent Opportunity

Potential Opportunity

Telling the future by looking at the past
assumes that conditions remain constant.
This is like driving a car
by looking in the rear view mirror.
– Herb Brody

73. Show R.E.S.P.E.C.T.

In the words of the great Otis Redding song,

R-e-s-p-e-c-t,
Find out what it means to me,
R-e-s-p-e-c-t
Take care of pleasin' me...

A few years ago I was hired to do sales training for one of the largest radio stations in LA. A few weeks before the event I took the station manager out for lunch to gather information about the staff. During our conversation I asked him how he got started in radio.

"For 25 years I waited on tables," he told me. "Then one day, the owner of this station—a regular at my table, asked if I would run his radio station.

He thought the owner was joking, but when it became clear that he was serious the waiter said, "I don't know how to do anything except wait on tables." But the wise executive replied, "You have all the qualities that I'm looking for. I can teach you what to do, but I can't teach you respect, decency, and good character."

I soon learned that he was the most revered station manager in LA. One of the reasons was abundantly clear—he showed respect to *everyone*. His decency paid off in a lucrative career and many admiring friends.

Let's look at what a lack of respect costs in hard cash. I once had an appointment with the manager of a financial investment firm to discuss sales training. On my way out, I asked the receptionist if she would validate my parking. "We only validate for customers. Office policy," she said.

While she knew I was there to discuss sales training, what she didn't realize was that part of my appointment was to discuss the possibility of working with one of their brokers to take over my orphaned accounts from another firm. Since the office's policy of conditional respect wasn't congruent with my own, I elected to take my business elsewhere.

There's *nothing* to be gained by being selective with your respect. Showing respect for others can be done by providing:

- deferential treatment
- appreciation and kindness
- showing honor, esteem, or consideration

Showing respect may be challenging when you run into abrasive or rude behavior, but assume you've caught that person at a stressful time. When this happens rise above the occasion. Apologize if appropriate as in, "I'm sorry this is a bad time for you." Offer to help if you can. Treat all of your contacts as though they were your most important customers. Every contact is priceless.

Who needs a healthy dose of your respect?

What first step will you take to show it?

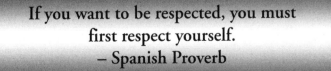

If you want to be respected, you must first respect yourself.
– Spanish Proverb

74. Visualize What You Want

One of the most important qualities of being human is our ability to imagine. Imagination is the creative force that allows us to see from within, "in-visioning" potential in our mind not only of *what* we want, but also *how* we might conduct ourselves in achieving it.

If a plan is the blueprint for getting things done, a vision is the architect's rendering of what it looks like in the end. A vision is simply a guiding image of a successful outcome. Visions provide two important functions in getting things done—clarity of direction and focused energy. If you could take a snapshot of the ideal future, you could see where to aim your efforts. Catching a glimpse of that potential moves passion to action. Visions sustain energy when the weight of what you want gets discouraging. They help to make the future believable. It's been said that if you can see it, you can achieve it.

Our ability to imagine the future allows us to step into it and literally pull ourselves in that desired direction. Visions also define the boundaries of our future—what is in the picture and what is *not*. If you see yourself working on straight referrals, your actions will support that image. Eventually you'll find that the idea is no longer a vision, but a reality.

Visualization Exercise:
Create a picture in your mind's eye of what your business would be like if you were working on straight referrals. Is the phone ringing off the hook? Where are you when all the calls are coming in? Do you need to hire additional support

124

systems? Are you delegating low priority chores? How will you manage the increase in your business? Close your eyes and imagine a future of steady business.

Now go to the master listing of this book and check off the most appropriate strategies, techniques, and attitudes that support your vision.

Next, prioritize those you've checked off and put the specific activities—what you will physically and/or mentally do—in your day planner.

Now begin and don't stop until you're up and running on straight referrals. It's been said that if you reach for the moon and miss, you'll get stars!

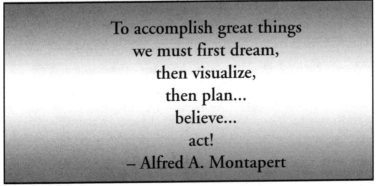

To accomplish great things
we must first dream,
then visualize,
then plan...
believe...
act!
– Alfred A. Montapert

75. Motivate Yourself!

This entry is for all those who want to build referrals but run into occasional motivational slumps. None of us can consistently sustain high levels of motivation. Life is so dynamic that in the normal course of events, we're bound to get discouraged once in awhile. We have to cultivate a good positive attitude by staying involved in activities that keep us buoyant. The challenge is this—when you're down in a slump, how long are you going to stay there?

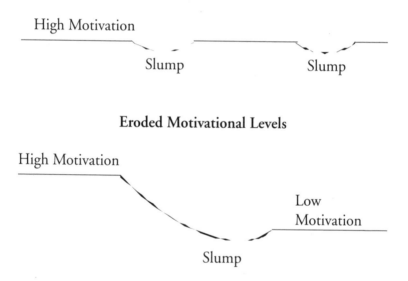

Normal Motivational Levels

High Motivation

Slump   Slump

Eroded Motivational Levels

High Motivation

Low
Motivation

Slump

Motivation is based on *motives* or the *reasons* why we do what we do. Our reasons in turn are based on the outcomes we expect or desire as a result of something taking place. If the consequences of something are positive, it tends to encourage or *reinforce* more of the same behavior. If the consequences are negative, it tends to extinguish the behavior. Positive and negative reinforcers can be used to change your motivation.

Positive Consequences Recycle Motivation

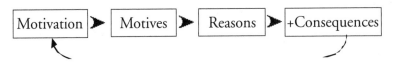

Negative Consequences Extinguish Motivation

The more positive the consequence, the greater the reinforcement (motivation) to keep performing the behavior. The more painful, the more likely the behavior will stop. Both positive and negative reinforcement can change behavior, but positive is the most powerful motivator for *sustaining* desireable behaviors. If we learn that asking for referrals produces results, for example, we'll tend to do more of it. If it doesn't work a few times, you may be tempted to stop asking. *Don't allow negative outcomes rode your motivation.* Here's the inside scoop—what motivates us most are outcomes that are positive, immediate, and certain (PIC) or negative, immediate, and certain (NIC). PICs and NICs control our behavior:

1. **Positive or Negative (P or N)**
   Will the outcome be a pleasurable or painful experience? This depends on your value system.

2. **Immediate or in the Future (I or F)**
   Will the consequence happen now or in the future? Outcomes that happen sooner are more motivating.

3. **Certain or Uncertain (C or U)**
   What's the probability that the outcome will occur? The more certain, the more motivating.

You may use PICs to set up situations that motivate yourself. The secret is to reap a reward as soon as possible to the behavior you want to keep doing. Here's how to implement PICs that will keep you going when the going gets tough.

1. Work in baby steps that provide small, successful payoffs leading to larger payoffs. Set up each small task to be a win (PIC) for you. Success is motivating and will keep you going.

2. Start on the easy part of a project first and work towards the more challenging tasks so that every task is more certain to be successful.

3. Give PICs to others. This could be a compliment or positive feedback. When you show appreciation to others, you'll tend to get appreciation back in return.

4. Look for opportunities to celebrate. Get together with others to relive challenges, lessons learned, and pay offs. After a task, reward yourself with *anything* special—lunch at a favorite restaurant, a gourmet cup of coffee, a walk outside, a hot bath, a day off.

5. Be good to yourself. Tell yourself that you can do anything you set your mind to. Be your own coach and give yourself a pep talk by only allowing positive thoughts. *You can do it!*

> **Ability is what you're capable of doing.**
> **Motivation determines what you do.**
> **Attitude determines how well you do it.**
> **– Lou Holtz**

76. Begin!

When my husband and his partner started their new business as free-lance writers, they sent out 100 mailers and followed up with "warm" calls. Both hated the experience and agreed that they needed to start their business with referrals. The alternative of frustrated cold calls and phone tag would have been discouraging and perhaps put them out of business before they got started.

For their first project, I gave them a copy of this manuscript to proofread and to glean ideas that could get them going. Within a week, they picked up six solid jobs and have two large projects pending. They used many ideas here, but some of the high-payoff activities that got them started were:

4. Partner: They set up reciprocal relationships with local graphic designers and were awarded one large job because of their expertise in a particular field.

22. Prospect Your Own Backyard: They called on current friends and acquaintances to get the word out. Work of mouth spread--someone knew someone who needed writers.

44. Find a Mentor: This duo works because my husband has a long resume of writing experience and his partner has graphic connections.

55. Prospect Your Past: They asked previous employers if they had any current projects that they wanted to farm out. They were given two web site jobs, part of which they will give back to the graphic designer.

You know the expression. One for the money, two for the show, three to get ready... three to get ready...three to get ready...

Don't procrastinate. Go to work at building your business now. Some of the ideas in this book are quick and easy to implement, like joining networking groups, sending out mailers, or sprucing up your professional image. Many of these simple ideas can bring you immediate results. Others will take a little more time and effort, like getting published or becoming known as an expert in your field. What's important is that you *begin.*

If you haven't been doing this all along, go through the checklist at the beginning of this book. Find the strategies that you can implement today and go right to work on them. Then develop plans for implementing more long-term strategies. Set definite dates in your day planner for following up and accomplishing your goals. *No more excuses.* You can do it and do it *now!*

Make *76 Ways to Build a Straight Referral Business, ASAP!* your business blueprint. Build it and they will buy. You'll create a foundation that can withstand the most rigorous economic workout, help the most number of people, and keep you financially fit for life $$$$$$$$$$$!

> *Everyday can be a blur;*
> *and every word,*
> *"I wish I were."*
> *But all we have is time today*
> *so waste it not on wishing away.*
> *DO IT NOW!*

Section 3
TEST YOUR SKILLS

The following scenes are designed to assess how well you've learned the ideas in this book. There are no wrong answers, but degrees of good, better, and best.

#1. Chamber of Commerce Networking Event

The local Chamber of Commerce is holding a networking event. Which of the following three people needs the most help with referral building skills?

> **Jean:** She is tastefully dressed in a three-piece, navy wool suit, white silk blouse, silver accessories, topped off with a radiant smile. Across the room she sees Nan, an investment banker high on her wish list of people to meet. Nan's already surrounded by three others, but Jean's confident she'll be able to seamlessly join the group. She approaches smiling and asks brightly, "May I join you?" The group nods with welcomes all around. Once inside, Jean's determined not to lose momentum. She quickly hands Nan a business card, her company prospectus, and starts talking about her new business.

Jean's referral ideas at work:

Jean's strengths:

Jean's weaknesses:

Bill: He sees Betty by the ice sculpture. At last year's event they were teamed on a scavenger hunt and they nearly won. Bill's an avid reader of the business page and has recently read of Betty's promotion to purchasing manager. He also knows that her company has no use for his services. He walks up behind Betty, who's busy looking over the iced shrimp, and says, "How's the hunting going? Bill Smith from last year's scavenger hunt." She turns, smiles, and—thanks to his introduction—immediately recognizes him. They shake hands, and Bill congratulates her on her promotion. She is impressed with his knowledge of current local business. He continues the conversation, focusing on learning her challenges and needs. He offers to call her the next day with some reputable referrals that will give her excellent service at competitive prices.

Bill's referral ideas at work:

Bill's strengths:

Bill's weaknesses:

Conrad: He had special business cards made up for this
event. One side contained all of his essential
business information. The flipside read:

Let's Play Six Degrees of Separation!

1   2   3   4   5   6

Game Rules:
See if we can find one person we know in common
by the time we've talked about six other people.
Prizes: Surprises!

Conrad sees a person he doesn't know (Jim) standing alone by the refreshment table. He walks over to Jim to initiate a conversation. He introduces himself and asks questions to find out more about Jim and his line of work. After a few minutes they learn that they both like to play golf and have relatives in Bakersfield. Then Conrad asks Jim for his business card. "I'd like to keep your card on file just in case anyone asks me for someone with your expertise. I'd be happy to pass your name along. By the way, I bet we know some people in common." He hands Jim one of his cards from his right jacket pocket and says, "Let's play, *Six Degrees of Separation.*" He goes on to explain the rules and they play the game for five minutes, discovering that they know both share mutual acquaintances with three other people.

Conrad's referral ideas at work:

Conrad's strengths:

Conrad's weaknesses:

Choose the one that needs the most help:

 Jean   Bill   Conrad

Chamber of Commerce Feedback:

Jean: She's got a lot of things going for her. She presents herself professionally and has the courage to approach what others might view as a closed circle. She's done her homework beforehand and knows who she wants to meet—Nan. Once she makes her way into the group, however, she blunders badly by taking over the group with her own self interests. At an appropriate break in the conversation, she could have excused herself from the group and asked Nan if she had a moment to meet with her. Jean might then begin her conversation with Nan by asking questions to qualify and match their interests such as, "Do you look for new businesses to represent, once in awhile? ("Yes.") Great. I've just started a new business that may be of interest your clients. Would you be interested in taking a look?" Jeans needs the most help.

Bill: He does a number of good things as well too. He's professional in his introduction by providing a cue and his name to refresh Betty's recollection of him without putting her in the embarrassing position of having to answer the question, "Do you remember me?" He also uses the business pages to stay on top of current events. His reading allowed him to make a connection with Betty that both acknowledged her success and showed a genuine interest in helping her as well. When we have the needs of others in mind first, the principle of reciprocity starts to work.

Conrad: He earns high points for standing out in the crowd with a unique business card and initiating conversations. He's using upside down thinking and positioning himself as an innovator. The game of *Six Degrees of Separation* is also a way to stimulate conversation for those who have difficulty knowing what to say after introductions. His game will begin to infuse the room with conversation, helping people to find similarities while increasing his memorability.

135

2. Computer Store:

In the next scenario, two of three people working in a local computer store are doing a good job at the extra effort that's so critical to referral building. Who is the one who could use improvement?

Sally: The social circle at Mrs. Hathaway's retirement village wants to get into cyberspace, and they've designated Mrs. Hathaway to lead the way. She comes into the store and tells Sally that she's got a computer, but doesn't know anything about modems. Sally shows her a couple of store models in a range of prices and explains the features and benefits of each. Mrs. H. tells Sally that she appreciates her effort, but she's afraid that when she gets home she won't be able to get it to work. Sally tells Mrs. H. that Internet service providers usually do a good job of helping you through your setup. But Mrs. H. can only think of the troubles she's had in the past with software installation. So Sally writes her home number on her business card and gives it to Mrs. H. "If you have any problems," she says, "give me a call anytime."

Sally's referral ideas at work:

Sally's strengths:

Sally's weaknesses:

136

Ben: Mr. Carlyle comes in and buys three new computers, two monitors, and a scanner. He compliments Ben on his product knowledge and tells him that he plans on sending more business his way. In fact, he tells Ben, he has five or six friends with similar equipment needs, and he'd be happy to refer them Ben's way if Ben can fatten the discount he's just given Mr. Carlyle. Ben does the math in his head—five times the order he's just filled. Wow! He knows that store policy won't support a bigger discount, but he can't pass up the opportunity to get all those referrals. He tells Mr. Carlyle to leave the order and that he'll deliver it after he's bought it with his employee discount.

Ben's referral ideas at work:

Ben's strengths:

Ben's weaknesses:

Leo: Max Diamond comes into the store shopping for an entrepreneur, with a scattered sales staff and a problem of getting everyone together for training. Leo suggests online training. Max is intrigued. He asks Leo to tell him more. Unfortunately Leo doesn't know a whole lot more. He just knows of online training from one his other customers, a bushy-haired guy named Gary. He tells Max that Gary has a new online training business and gives Max a copy of Gary's business card. Max thanks Leo and heads out the door with his software.

Leo's referral ideas at work:

Leo's strengths:

Leo's weaknesses:

Which one blundered? Please check one:

 Sally   Ben   Leo

Computer Store Feedback:

Sally: She's not just a go-getter but a go-giver, too. By her extending her services beyond the call of duty, all those folks in the retirement village will be lining up to buy modems from her—maybe computers too. Sally could be entering a nest of referrals that lead her to every interested buyer in the area—all because she added value to her service and did the right thing for her customer—provided peace of mind through personalized service.

Ben: What's wrong with this picture? He made the sale. He showed he knew his product. He knows the store policy on discounts. Why'd he compromise his ethics by purchasing Carlyle's order with his employee discount? This could back-fire and make Carlyle reluctant to send referrals—working with an unethical sales person would be a bad reflection on *him*. With no assurances that Ben's ever going to see those five or six referrals, he put his job and reputation at risk. Ben needs help.

Leo: As the ball players like to say, he stayed within himself. He gave Max only the information he knew and didn't get in over his head trying to explain the technical details of online training. In addition, he used a little upside down thinking to get out of his sales role, change his perspective and do some creative match making—putting two of his customers to-gether. In doing so, he probably doubled his chances for referrals—from Max and from Gary.

#3: Asking Directly:

In the next three scenarios, each of our fictional characters is asking for a referral. Some sales people are very effective at asking. Many are not. Which one in the following group is *most* effective?

Felix: Once Mr. and Mrs. Henderson have signed for their new life insurance policies, Felix asks them to bring in the kids for a surprise. When the kids arrive, he astonishes the entire family with tickets to the biggest amusement park in all of Prospect Hollow. With the kids dancing around the house for joy, Felix then asks the senior Hendersons who else they think would like to have their insurance assessed.

John: After selling the Crowes their new vacuum cleaner, John says, "Boy, you folks have been real lifesavers. If it weren't for you, I'd never have made my quota this month. That could've cost me my job. I sure hope it doesn't happen next month because I've got a ton of bills due…including my daughter's tuition. I'll be honest with you, it sure would help if you could give me a couple of referrals to call on."

Margaret: When she comes by the Winslows to pick up the final payment for their beautiful solarium, she asks if they've shown any of their family or friends their new addition. When she learns that they have, and that the feedback has been glowing, she asks her customers if they can think of anyone in the group who would be interested in taking a look at adding all-weather living space to their home.

Which one is most effective? Please check one:

Felix   John   Margaret

Asking Directly Feedback:

Felix has crossed the line by offering gifts. When given immediately after a sale and in conjunction with asking for referrals, the gift looks like a bribe. He has placed his new customers in an embarrassing and compromised situation where they may feel that they *have* to give referrals to pay for his gift. He may take home a few referrals, but he has undermined his professionalism and ethics.

John has shamelessly tried to exploit his customers' sympathies and his own shortcomings to gain a referral. Did we mention appearing desperate?

Margaret uses a conversational technique to open the possibility of referrals. If her customers are happy with their purchase and Margaret's professionalism, they'll likely provide her with access to potential customers in their circle of influence. She could

4: Asking Indirectly:

This scenario is a little less direct in its approach. In this hypothetical café, there are three real estate agents and their respective clients having coffee at three different tables. Two of the agents are doing a good job at laying the groundwork for referrals; one is less effective.

141

Lucy: Over a mocha latte, she explains that client satisfaction is very important to her. To help provide the best service, she asks if they would be willing to answer a few questions about their recent transaction that would help her to fulfill her promise. When they agree, she puts a self-addressed, stamped post card on the table and asks them to drop it in the mail after they've filled it out. The questions include the following, on a rating scale of 1-5:

___ 1. How would you rate my understanding of the kind of home you were looking to buy?

___ 2. How would you rate my explanation of your financing options?

___ 3. How would you rate my attentiveness to your needs?

___ 4. What one thing would you recommend for improvement in my services?

___ 5. Would you recommend my services to others?

___ 6. Who do you know that may be looking to buy or sell real estate?

Lucy's strengths:

Lucy's weaknesses:

Fran: She really wasn't looking forward to this meeting after the difficult escrow her clients, the Cohns, went through. A summer intern at the office had failed to submit the Cohns paperwork on time, extending their escrow by 30 days and jeopardizing the sale. Over coffee Fran repeats an earlier apology. She also tells the Cohns that their experience has prompted her company to review its supervisory policies in regards to interns. At the end, the Cohns ask Fran if she knows of a good faux artist. Fran does. His work is first rate. Because she wants to end the meeting on a high note, Fran avoids mentioning that this faux artist is also notoriously unreliable.

Fran's strengths:

Fran's weaknesses:

Barbara: Her buyers are so pleased with their new home that they shower Barbara with gratitude. She thanks them for their appreciation and adds, "Wasn't the escrow company terrific? They're so vital in getting a transaction done without snags." Then Barbara adds, "We're fortunate to have so many highly skilled people on our team. All the pieces work together to help people find the right home. We're very fortunate to have so many repeat clients who refer us to their friends. If there's anything we can ever do to help you again or someone you know, please don't hesitate to call."

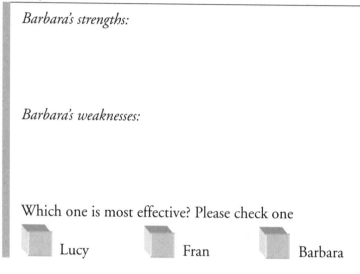

Barbara's strengths:

Barbara's weaknesses:

Which one is most effective? Please check one

☐ Lucy   ☐ Fran   ☐ Barbara

Asking Indirectly Feedback:

Lucy: She's created a good, low-key request for information. Her buyers can walk away with the referral card. If they choose to fill it out with her then and there, she'll get immediate feedback. When she gets to the question on referrals, she'll have opened the door to potentially obtaining new leads. It could feel a bit awkward though if not handled properly.

Fran: She does almost everything right—the coffee was great; the apology sincere; the admission of error by her company, and the fact that it's using the Cohn's misfortune to correct an internal problem may have helped to restore good faith. She admitted to the mistake and that shows good character. Her downfall was recommending a painter she knew who had a bad reputation. That'll probably come back to haunt her and cost her future referrals.

Barbara: Here's a woman who has her ducks in a row. At the end of the meeting, her buyers see that she operates within a solid gold network of professionals. They'll not only be telling their friends to see Barbara to buy a house, but also remember Barbara when they want expert advice on any real estate related questions—new loans, vacation home, rentals, reliable pest control, interior designers, gardeners, electricians.

#5. Wine Tasting: Part 1 of 2

Nan is a highly motivated investment advisor who's put her last name, "Brandy," to work by familiarizing her clients with fine wines. Three times a year she invites her clients and prospects to a wine tasting at her friend Tony's wine cellar. She doesn't need new business, but wants to keep her funnel full of new prospects. She visualizes a packed house of 75 and often reaches that goal.

While the folks sample Tony's new wines, Nan explains her range of services and gives investment tips. She also alerts her guests to new information that she posts on her website weekly. During one of these events, she learns of the imminent retirement of Malcolm Holmes, her main competitor. So Nancy takes a case of vintage wine, boxes up each of 48 bottles with a note that reads, "If you want to learn more about wine or investments, please call me at 760-639-4020." She then sends the bottles to Malcolm's top 50 clients.

Soon the calls start coming in, including one from Ford Graham. He loved the wine and wants to meet with her. Their meeting goes so well that they agree to write an article for Ford's industry newsletter entitled, "When Your Investment Advisor Retires before You Do."

Nan has learned to make herself very visible. How many total referral strategies is she using? _____ (Answer on next page.)

Which of the following groups best sum up the vintage referral building strategies she used?

Cabernet

> Partner
> Market with Your Customers
> Adopt Orphan Accounts
> Visualize What you Want

Champagne

> Partner
> Brand Yourself
> Network
> Motivate Yourself

Bordeaux

> Partner
> Mix Business with Pleasure
> Get Published
> "Click" with Your Silent Partner

Chardonnay

> Partner
> Expand Your Circle of Influence
> Have a Creative Lookout Tower
> Network with Your Competition

If you checked them all, you're on the fast track to success! Nan used all these strategies plus many more.
(Answer from previous page: at least 48)

You've probably noticed that many of these ideas overlap. You can see that by doing a few things you can accomplish a great deal. This helps you further leverage your efforts into successful outcomes.

Wine Tasting: Part 2 of 2

It's been a very good year. Not only has Nan captured 75% of Malcolm Holmes's previous clients, but her article, "When Your Investment Advisor Retires before You Do" has grown into a book. She's also followed in Malcolm's footsteps by becoming president of the Chamber of Commerce.

Before giving the opening speech, she stands in the middle of a small, admiring group at the annual Chamber mixer talking to them about her favorite Italian wines. Suddenly a woman named Jean introduces herself to the group, hands Nan her business card, and says, "Oh, Ms. Brandy, I'm so glad to meet you. I'm just starting my own business and I think it will make a terrific investment opportunity for some of your clients...."

Well, we met Jean in the first scenario, so we already know that she has a few things to learn about working for referrals. But not so for Nan. She's soaring.

Which of the following has been most crucial to her long-term referral building strategies?

> Surrounding herself with admirers.
>
> Becoming a wine expert.
>
> Being seen and heard.
>
> Staying in touch.

Here are my suggestions:

Admirers: They're not a strategy; they're the outcome of a good strategy.

Wine expert: Yes, that certainly has helped. But in this situation, her reputation is beyond that.

Seen and heard: This is important, but only if you have something of value to offer. Being out there isn't enough to create genuine success in serving others.

Staying in touch: Eureka! How many ways can you find to connect? Nan found dozens. This one looks like a lifetime of work, but that's the point. Your *career* is not your life; your *life* is your career. The people you meet, the relationships you build, and the people you help will detemine its quality. Go out there and "touch someone!"

#6. Prospecting:
Three of the following four people would make very good prospects for you. One of them wouldn't. Which one is that?

Mack: Head of the service department at your company. He keeps thorough records on the repair history of your products and has a great reputation with customers.

148

Jeremy: One of your current clients. He made one of the biggest buys in your career, but unfortunately got himself financially over his head in that transaction and has regretted the buy ever since.

Mrs. Grunwald: Your old high school English teacher. *Mr. Grunwald* is the new executive VP of a company you've been trying to do business with for over a year.

Ellen: Your neighbor. She has no personal need for your product line but she's President of a large, active business women's group

*So many possibilities, but one of them is problematical. Whom did you choose?*_____

Here are my suggestions:

Mack: This mine is practically an evergreen. It's a constantly renewable source of referrals.

Jeremy: No go! A current client like Jeremy would have been a good source for referrals under better circumstances. At this point, however, he's not about to lead any of his friends and associates into the same fix he's in.

Mrs. Grunwald: She's always happy to hear a voice from the past and is eager to hear what you're up to these days. This is a natural lead-in to meeting Mr. Grunwald.

Ellen: You've struck it rich here! She knows you and knows there are a number of women in her group who need your product and services.

149

About the Author
Lorna Riley

Named "Consummate Speaker of the Year," Lorna Riley is the President and CEO of the American Training Association, OTC Learning Solutions Inc., and one of the elite international productivity presenters. Having increased sales by 600%, she is the winner of five productivity and speaker awards and author of five books including *Achieving Results, Quest for Your Best: Four Stages to Finding Fulfillment in a Challenging World,* and *Off-the-Chart Leadership Results™.* She is the creator of three audio albums on Time Management, Memory Management, Leadership, Communication, 30 sales programs, and 60 productivity programs. She is a frequent contributor to trade publications and featured in national magazines, radio, and TV. Organizations that want results delivered with energy, humor, cutting-edge content, and interaction may reach Lorna Riley at:

760-639-4020   lorna @lornariley.com
www.lornariley.com

Lorna Riley has had work experience in public education, banking, insurance, retail sales, publishing, direct sales, advertising, computer graphics, and music. This diversity has given Lorna a unique perspective on the common denominator of success. Lorna has earned the Certified Speaking Professional designation, an honored classification held by less than 8% of professional speakers.

> **Call now for Lorna's sales and leadership assessments, based on 60 years combined research of over 80,000 managers in 400 companies.**

√ High-Impact √ Motivational
√ Results-Driven Training
by the American Training Assoc.
760-639-4020

COMMUNICATION
Listening Skills
Presentation Skills
Interpersonal Communication
Assertiveness Training
Behavioral/Social Styles
Customer Service
Telephone Skills
Calming Upset Customers
Team Building
Train the Trainer
Conflict Management

TIME MANAGEMENT
Change Management
Missions and Vision
Goal Setting
Organizational Skills
Quest for Your Best
Preventing Job Burnout
Balancing Home/Career
Stress Management
Time Management
Life Management
Delegation Skills

SALES
Basic/Advanced Selling
Consultative Selling
Relationship Selling
Major Account Selling
Telemarketing
Negotiations
Referral Building
Territory Management
Psychology of Selling

THINKING SKILLS
Attitude Adjustments
Psychology of Motivation
Motivating Employees
Problem Solving
Strategic Planning
Decision Making
Creativity/Innovation
Memory Management
Value Clarification

LEADERSHIP
Off-the-Chart Leadership Results™
Management Training
Supervisory Training
Leadership for Women
Empowerment
Assessments

CONTACT:
American Training Assn.
2455 Flametree Lane,
Vista, CA 92084
760-639-4020
www.lornariley.com

151